A HISTORY TODAY BOOK

RICHARD III
A Medieval Kingship

A HISTORY TODAY BOOK

RICHARD III
A Medieval Kingship

EDITED BY
John Gillingham

COLLINS & BROWN

First published in Great Britain in 1993
by Collins & Brown Limited
Letts of London House
Great Eastern Wharf
Parkgate Road
London SW11 4NQ

1 3 5 7 9 8 6 4 2

British Library Cataloguing-in-Publication Data:
A catalogue record for this book
is available from the British Library.

ISBN 1 85585 100 8 (hardback edition)
ISBN 1 85585 203 9 (paperback edition)

Filmset by Spectrum City, London
Printed and bound in Great Britain by
Hillman Printers (Frome) Ltd

CONTENTS

Chapter 1

INTRODUCTION:
INTERPRETING RICHARD III

John Gillingham

RICHARD III REIGNED for two years, two months and one day. Yet the impact of his reign on prevailing perceptions of English history is out of all proportion to its brevity. Undeniably this is chiefly because of the accusation that he murdered the Princes in the Tower and because of the profound and timeless issues of life and death, guilt and innocence, justice and injustice, which that accusation raises. As I shall argue later, these are issues which have important implications for our understanding of the historian's role. But the fact that Richard's life ended when it did also means that his reign enjoys another kind of prominence — the result of the '1485 factor', the notion that the personal tragedies which afflicted the 'generation of 1485' had a wider historical significance, that they amounted to nothing less than a fundamental crisis of the political system.

Ever since the tenth century when the kingdom of England came into existence, and with the brief exception of the Commonwealth period in the seventeenth century, there has been a monarchy in England, and a hereditary monarchy at that. From the perspective of the twentieth century, this thousand-year monarchy has been one of the most characteristic and enduring features of our history. Yet in 1485, or so it is widely believed, the monarchy was under threat. Ralph Griffiths, for example, in the *Oxford Illustrated History of Britain* suggests that 'The Wars of the Roses came close to denying the

1

hereditary basis of the English monarchy.' In the same volume, John Guy goes still further, arguing that although the wars 'had done negligible permanent damage to agriculture, trade and industry', they 'had unquestionably undermined confidence in monarchy as an institution'. Thus, in his words, 'the quest for political stability at the end of the fifteenth century remained of paramount importance to future progress'. Perhaps no one any longer believes that 1485 marks the end of 'medieval' and the birth of 'modern' England, but for historians of monarchy the date clearly retains much of its mythic power. And, for historians of Richard III's reign, this is a view which raises important problems of interpretation.

If Henry Tudor faced a situation in which confidence in monarchy had been undermined, then what had undermined it? Was it the result of a protracted crisis which started in the 1450s and continued right through to the late 1480s, an interconnected sequence of events which historians have labelled the Wars of the Roses? If this is so, then Richard's reign represents no more than a brief coda, and, however bloody, can constitute only a small part of the problem. (Obviously it is impossible to accept Shakespeare's portrait of Richard as the evil genius whose malice and cunning overshadow the whole period from the first Battle of St Albans in 1455 onwards.) However, the more positive assessment of the last dozen years (1471–83) of Edward IV's reign in recent scholarship has led to the conclusion that what happened in 1483 and after was quite different from, and essentially unrelated to, the struggles of the years between 1455 and 1471. Whether historians of the Wars of the Roses distinguish three separate wars (e.g. 1455–61, 1469–71 and 1483–87) — as I did writing in 1981 — or whether, like A. J. Pollard, we prefer to distinguish only two (1459–71 and 1483–87), what these views have in common is the conviction that the crisis that began in 1483 was distinct from what went before.

It is, of course, very difficult to measure levels of confidence, or lack of it. But if we interrogate Sir John Fortescue, the most distinguished political thinker of the day, then it is clear that in the 1470s he was as full of confidence as a minster making an electioneering speech at a party conference. In his most famous treatise, *The Governance of England*, he writes of the English monarchy as the best political system in the world — in need of reform certainly, but still the best (*see boxes on pages 4–5 and 6–7*).

At times it is hard not to be amused by Fortescue's absurdly patriotic sentiments — for example, when he compared the incidence of robbery in England, France and Scotland — but he clearly expected his words to evoke a sympathetic response from his contemporaries. And Fortescue was no ivory-tower theorist. In the 1470s he was an old man with decades of practical experience behind him, experience of both government office and political exile. His treatise shows that in the 1470s there were people well aware of the need for reform, and that there was a lively debate about the precise shape which that reform should take. It is interesting too that the chief plank of Fortescue's reform programme — the resumption of former royal estates and the effective landed endowment of the Crown — was one which was actually being put into practice. As David Starkey has put it, 'the revenue base of the Crown was transformed and the method of revenue administration radically altered — all within the last decade of Edward IV's reign' (in *Revolution Reassessed*, 1986). Neither in thought nor in deed was this a monarchy which was being undermined.

Moreover, Edward IV had a very strong hereditary claim to his crown. Admittedly the House of York had done very little to press its right to the throne in the years after 1399, but that objection had been answered by Edward's father in 1460: 'For though right for a time rest and be put to silence, yet it rotteth not nor shall not perish.' By contrast, when Richard claimed the throne by hereditary right, he did so on grounds which most contemporaries found incredible and shocking. The result was the 'doubts and seditious language' which the rehearsal of Richard's title in the Parliament of January 1484 was explicitly intended to remove. But apparently the doubts would not go away. Three months later, the London guilds were summoned in order that they might listen to yet another declaration of Richard's right and title. As for Henry Tudor, his hereditary claim to the throne was so weak

3

The Governance of England

J OHN FORTESCUE was a very distinguished lawyer and political thinker. In 1442 he became Chief Justice of the King's Bench and was knighted soon afterwards. Loyalty to Henry VI and Queen Margaret resulted in his exile for several years but in the early 1470s he became reconciled to Edward IV. In this, his last work, written in the early 1470s, Fortescue retains the key distinction of his political thought between a *regnum regale* (typically France) and a *regnum politicum et regale* (typically England). In the former, the king can change the laws of his kingdom at his pleasure and can also impose taxes without consulting his people; in the latter he cannot. So, Fortescue explains, when 'England's men made war in France' the French king

> set *tailles* and other impositions upon the commons without the assent of the three estates; but yet he would not set any such charges, nor hath set, upon the nobles for fear of rebellion. And because the commons there, though they have grouched, have not rebelled — nor are they bold enough to rebel — the French kings have yearly set such charges upon them, and so augmented the same charges, that the said commons be impoverished and destroyed ... They drink water, they eat apples, with bread right brown

(*see box on page 8*) that he had very good reasons for not talking about it in precise terms — exactly the opposite of the strategy which Richard of York had adopted.

In other words, the threat to the hereditary basis of the monarchy came not from the Wars of the Roses in general, but from the crisis which was precipitated in 1483. In the years up to 1483, Edward IV's eldest son had been expected to succeed his father and had, in consequence, been proclaimed king immediately after his father's death, so when Richard took over he was inevitably disturbing the smooth and even flow of predictable events. What is more, by launching a savage attack on the nature of his brother's rule, claiming that it had done serious damage to the fabric of society, Richard was using language calculated to shake people's faith in the achievement of the House of

made of rye; they eat no flesh but if it be right seldom a little lard, or of the
entrails and heads of beasts slain for the nobles and merchants of the land.

After more heart-rending words on the terrible plight of the French
people, he concludes:

Verily they live in the most extreme poverty and misery and yet they dwell
in one of the most fertile realms of the world. Wherefore the French king
hath not men of his own realm able to defend it, except the nobles, which
do not bear such impositions . . . by which cause the said king is compelled
to make his armies and retinues for the defence of his land of strangers, as
Scots, Spaniards, Aragonese, Germans and of other nations, or else all his
enemies might overrun him . . . Lo, this is the fruit of his *Ius regale*.

If the realm of England, which is an isle, and therefore may not lightly
get succour of other lands, were ruled under such a law, and under such a
prince, it would be a prey to all other nations that would conquer, rob or
devour it . . . But blessed be God, this land is ruled under a better law; and
therefore the people thereof be not in such penury . . . but have all things
necessary to the sustenance of nature. Wherefore they be mighty, and able
to resist the adversaries of this realm, and beat other realms that do, or
would do them wrong. Lo this is the fruit of *Ius politicum et regale* under
which we live.

York. Reading Richard's denunciations of a regime in which he had
played a leading role (*see box on page 9*), it is hard not to think that if,
after 500 years of existence, the institution of hereditary monarchy was
now endangered, then it was Richard himself who had brought this
about.

For whatever his motives may have been, it was Richard who, in
1483, chose the path and the rhetoric of destabilization. Why did he do
this? What did he fear or hope to gain? What sort of a man was he?
Why did some people support and others oppose him? If his reign was
indeed 'traumatic for the English policy', as Michael Bennett claims
in *The Battle of Bosworth*, then these are questions which matter.

Thus it is not in the least surprising that there should be no king
of England who aroused and continues to arouse stronger passions

FORTESCUE'S ENGLAND: A LAND OF WEALTHY
COMMONERS AND BOLD ROBBERS

THE FOLLOWING PASSAGES, also from *The Governance of England*, throw intriguing light on one of the topics of political debate in later fifteenth-century England. So far as Fortescue was concerned, even English criminals were superior to those from less happy lands:

> ... some men have said that it were good for the king that the commons of England were made poor like the commons of France. For then they would not rebel ... as the commons of France do not, nor may do for they have no weapons, no armour nor the goods to buy it withal. Forsooth these folk consider little the good of the realm of England, whereof the might standeth most upon archers, which be no rich men. And if they were made more poor than they be, they should not have wherewith to buy them bows, arrows, jacks or any other armour or defence ... wherefore the making poor of the commons, which is the making poor of our archers, shall be the destruction of the greatest might of our realm. And how then, if a mighty man made a rising, should he be repressed when all the commons be so poor ... and by that reason not help the king with fighting?
>
> What then would befall if all the commons were poor? Truly it is like that this land should be like unto the realm of Bohemia where the commons for poverty rose upon the nobles and made all their goods to be held in common.
>
> Again, it is the king's honour, and also his office, to make his realm

— both for and against. During his reign, no king faced more determined opposition; yet in this century no king's posthumous reputation has been more fiercely defended.

Many thoughtful people will certainly regard my interpretation of Richard as just yet another hatchet job, the pathetic fag-end of the tradition of Sir Thomas More and Shakespeare. These passions, and the moral issues of justice and injustice on which they are based, confront historians with an extraordinarily sharply defined example of one of their usual dilemmas. Should they — can they — avoid rich ... God give him grace to augment his realm in riches, wealth and prosperity. But our commons be rich and therefore they sometimes give to their king fifteenths and tenths, sometimes other great subsidies, as he hath need for the good and defence of his realm. How great a subsidy it was when the realm gave to their king a five year fifteenth and tenth, and other subsidies for five years! This they might not have done if they had been impoverished by their king as be the commons in France. Nor hath such a grant been made by any realm of Christendom of which any chronicle maketh mention. For they have not so much freedom in their own goods, nor be treated by such favourable laws as we be.

Fortescue's analysis of course confronts him with the problem of explaining why the impoverished French people did not rebel as the English would have done — 'like unto the realm of Bohemia'. His answer was the confidently patriotic one that the French 'lack heart and courage, which no Frenchman hath like unto an Englishman'. His evidence?

It is right seldom that Frenchmen be hanged for robbery, for they have no heart to do so terrible an act. There are more men hanged in one year in England for robbery and manslaughter than in seven years for such crimes in France. In Scotland seven years can go by without a single man being hanged for robbery. And yet they are often hanged for larceny, and stealing of goods in the absence of the owner thereof. But their hearts serve them not to take any man's property while he is present and will defend it . . . But the Englishman is of another courage . . . wherefore it is not poverty but lack of heart and cowardice that keepeth the Frenchman from rising.

passing moral judgments? When interpreting evidence, some of which was itself the product of the contemporary war of propaganda, should they — can they — remain detached and impartial commentators, steering a middle course between the Scylla and Charybdis of the pro- and anti-Richards? When assessing Richard should we apply 'medieval' or 'modern' standards? Indeed, did people have different standards 'then' — or were they just like 'us'?

Since different historians think differently about these matters, I have asked seven historians, all of them acknowledged experts on the

THE DECLARATION OF HENRY VII'S TITLE

IN THE FIRST PARLIAMENT of his reign (November 1485) Henry VII had his title to the throne declared in what Ralph Griffiths has aptly described as 'phrases of resounding emptiness'.

To the pleasure of Almighty God, the wealth, prosperity and surety of this realm of England, to the singular comfort of all the king's subjects of the same, and in avoiding of all ambiguities and questions, be it ordained, established and enacted by authority of this present parliament that the inheritance of the crowns of the realms of England and France, with all the pre-eminence and dignity royal to the same pertaining, and all other lordships to the king belonging beyond the sea, with the appurtenances thereto in any wise due or pertaining, be, rest, remain, and abide in the most royal person of our now sovereign lord King Harry the VIIth, and in the heirs of his body lawfully come, perpetually with the grace of God so to ensure and in none other.

late fifteenth century, to consider seven different aspects of Richard's life and reign. As will be obvious, they do not all share the same view of Richard. Nor — although it is often maintained that women take a more charitable view of Richard than do men — do the five male contributors take one line and the two women another. (I make this observation only because Audrey Williamson, author of the popular *Mystery of the Princes. An investigation into a supposed murder*, wrote that 'one occasionally has an odd feeling that male historians are not human beings at all but have drifted here from outer space.')

In their different ways, all the contributors throw a great deal of light, and sometimes entirely new perspectives, on Richard III's life and reign. Yet, at the end of it all, there can be no denying that Richard himself remains an enigma — and probably always will. Of all the kings of England he is at once the most abject failure and the most extraordinary success. Even his staunchest defenders have to admit that getting himself killed in battle in August 1485 was a failure, one which dragged down with him both the house of York and his own

RICHARD'S ATTACK ON HIS BROTHER'S GOVERNMENT

THE PARLIAMENTARY ACT of January 1484 which confirmed Richard's title to the throne incorporated the text of the bill presented to him on 26 June 1483 asking him to take the crown. The bill, after outlining how, once upon a time, 'this land many years stood in great prosperity, honour, and tranquillity', then moves on to deal with Edward IV's reign, and it does so in vitriolic terms:

> Over this more especially we consider how that in the time of the reign of King Edward IV lately deceased, the order of all politic rule was perverted, the laws of God and of God's church, and also the laws of nature and of England, and also the laudable customers and liberties of the same, wherein every Englishman is inheritor, broken, subverted and held in contempt, against all reason and justice, so that this land was ruled by self-will and pleasure, fear and dread, all manner of equity and laws laid aside and despised, whereof ensued many inconveniences and mischiefs, as murders, extortions and oppressions, namely, of poor and impotent people, so that no man was sure of his life, land, livelihood, nor of his wife, daughter, nor servant, every good maiden and woman standing in dread to be ravished and defouled.

The bill's explanation for this allegedly atrocious state of affairs was Edward IV's style of kingship:

> ... when such as had the rule and governance of this land, delighting in adulation and flattery and led by sensuality and concupiscence, followed the counsel of persons insolent, vicious and of inordinate avarice, despising the counsel of good, virtuous and prudent persons, the prosperity of this land daily decreased, so that felicity was turned to misery, and prosperity into adversity, and the order of policy, and of the law of God and man, confounded.

Such passages as this render Richard III very vulnerable to the charge of hypocrisy for in 1483 he was either putting forward spurious justifications for his coup or he really believed what he was now saying about his brother's regime. But, if the latter, then he had spent many years not only concealing his feelings, but even actively co-operating with a government which he believed to be corrupt.

followers, those who had supported him loyally through two difficult years and looked to him to protect and promote their interests. In his own lifetime Richard failed to live up to a king's most fundamental responsibilities: to ensure the survival of himself, his dynasty and his followers.

Yet no other king can match his posthumous success. No other king has in modern times attracted so many followers, women as well as men, determined to show that he was overthrown by a malign conspiracy and not through any terrible fault on his part — that if he had a failing it was that he was too merciful for the violent age in which he lived. One direct consequence of his failure was that, as Stubbs pointed out, 'he left none behind him whose duty or care it was to attempt his vindication.' Thus he was left to the tender mercies of the Tudors, his opponents in battle, and this in turn led to the feeling that he had been hard done by, a feeling that could be freely expressed once the Tudors were out of the way. And, as P. W. Hammond demonstrates, from the early seventeenth century onwards there have always been some who doubted the traditional Tudor image of the murderous tyrant. Occasionally societies have been founded in the name of one or other king, but none of these societies can hold a candle to the astonishing achievement of the Richard III Society. Founded in 1924, as the Fellowship of the White Boar, and then revived in the 1950s, the Society continues to go from strength to strength. It now publishes not only a newsletter, the *Ricardian Bulletin*, but also its own academic journal, *The Ricardian,* devoted to reassessing late fifteenth-century history 'in the belief that many features of the traditional accounts of the character and career of Richard III are neither supported by sufficient evidence nor reasonably tenable'. It is a measure of the Society's achievement that two of the contributors to this volume, Anne Sutton, editor of *The Ricardian*, and P. W. Hammond, former editor and current research officer, are among its most distinguished officers.

Central to any and every view of Richard is our interpretation of the events of 1483, surely the most controversial year in English history. Did Richard have any justification, either legal or political, for taking the throne? Was he responsible for the deaths of his nephews? Not everyone will agree with Colin Richmond's answers to these questions, and he would be the last to expect them to. The nature of the direct evidence is such that no absolutely certain answer can be given to either of these questions. All answers to them remain matters of judgement and interpretation.

Nevertheless, there can be no doubt that the 'mystery of the princes' lies at the heart of the enigma of Richard III. If Richard was guilty of monstrous crimes, then we are faced with the enigma of a man who after years of loyal service to his brother suddenly turned against his brother's children. It is against this background that Michael Hicks assesses Richard's early life. On the other hand, if he was not guilty why did so many men so swiftly decide to take up arms against him? It is because direct evidence of his guilt or innocence is lacking that every aspect of Richard's life and reign, indeed every aspect of late fifteenth-century history, has taken on a special and peculiar interest. For instance, does the culture of Richard's court show him to be a thoroughly conventional king, his interests, in Anne Sutton's words, 'probably representative of the interests of his average courtier'? If so, could such an 'ordinary' king have carried out such extraordinary crimes? In this sense almost every scrap of information has within it the potential that it might shed some indirect light on the courtroom drama. Did he, or didn't he? Guilty, or not guilty?

But to see history, even the history of 1483, as a courtroom drama is to adopt an approach which makes some historians distinctly uneasy. They believe that it is no part of their job to pass judgements on individuals. As David Knowles, one of the twentieth century's most distinguished scholars, wrote 'the historian is not a judge, still less a hanging judge.' Reluctance to act as the judge, combined with an acute awareness of the limitations of the evidence, has led to a kind of accommodation between professional historians and Ricardians in recent years. We have been urged to set aside what cannot be known, in order to focus instead on other aspects of Richard's reign*. This has contributed to a rehabilitation of Richard, to seeing him as a ruler who,

---

*However, the most recent book on him, a fine study by A. J. Pollard, accurately entitled *Richard III and the Princes in the Tower*, reverts to the old-fashioned practice of putting the fate of the princes at the heart of the matter.

in Michael Bennett's words (*The Battle of Bosworth*), 'came close to the model of English kingship. He had the makings of a great soldier-king, a generous patron of the Church, a fearless champion of justice and a far-sighted advocate of the "common weal".' How well does this judgement stand up to the Michael Jones's appraisal of Richard as a soldier, to Rosemary Horrox's penetrating analysis of Richard's government and to Alexander Grant's re-examination of Richard's foreign policy — a subject which, as he shows, has been neglected for far too long ?

According to Charles Ross in what will long remain the standard, scholarly life of Richard (*Richard III*), 'attention to ultimately in-soluble problems of historical detection ignores an entire dimension of critical evaluation of his life and reign. Richard was born into a violent age.' Ross then, after listing instances of killings and political murders which 'taught Richard lessons in arbitrary procedures', concludes that 'to put Richard into the context of his own violent age is not to make him morally a better man, but at least it makes him more under-standable. In the climate of high politics of his own day, his mistakes may then be seen as errors of judgement rather than moral failures.'

That people should be judged in the context of their own times is, of course, a historians' commonplace. At all costs, avoid anachronism. As an approach to understanding those who lived in the past, it can be — sometimes has been — used to excuse or justify individuals. They were not to blame. It was 'the age in which they lived'. The danger with this approach is that it can all too easily go hand in hand with chronocentrism — the assumption that our age is a superior one, that because there has been technological development there has also been a more general cultural progress. As a result, we see our-selves as being more enlightened and more civilized than the people of the past, especially those people whom we designate 'medieval'. (This assumption about the 'medieval' past tends to be reinforced every time commentators refer to a practice or institution of which they disapprove — often in 'less-developed' parts of the world — as being 'positively medieval'). The link between chronocentrism and the insistence that we should see the past on 'its' own terms, not on 'ours', is often easy to detect. The early nineteenth-century historian, Sharon Turner, suggested that, similarly placed, most of Richard's contemporaries would have acted very much as he did, for, as he reminded his readers, Richard 'did not live in an age of modern moral sensibilities'. There was clearly a similar assumption in the avowedly authoritative *Cambridge Medieval History* in which C. H. Williams wrote of Richard that 'the more we visualise him as a man of his own times, the more satisfying that view will appear to be . . . Sentiment was not a fifteenth-century virtue, and neither Richard nor his contemporaries cared much about the fate of those whom business or politics threw in their way.'

But to say that Richard was born into a violent age does not take us very far. As with any age, the real question is which forms of violence were widely regarded as regrettably acceptable and which were not. By 1483 it is clear that men might be killed by the victor if they were captured in arms and that a king's political enemies might be judicially murdered, that is put on trial and executed for some alleged treason. But, even by these standards, what Richard did in having Hastings, Rivers, Vaughan and Grey put to death in 1483 was not usual late fifteenth-century violence. Then again there is the 'mystery of the princes' — the belief, already widespread by the autumn of 1483, that Richard had killed his nephews. Chronocentrist assumptions have enabled even this to be played down — assuming that he did have them killed, Jeremy Potter, for example, argued that 'it is improbable that many men and women stood aghast at the possibility that the deposed boy king had been murdered' on the grounds that 'the fifteenth century was a raw age, lived in the shadow of death from the moment of birth. Children were plentiful and infant mortality was high . . .' (*Good King Richard?*, 1983). But the common notion that 'medieval' people took what was by 'our' standards, a callous view of children, a notion popularized in the writings of the influential French historical sociologist, Philippe Ariès, is simply untrue, just another example of chronocentrism in operation. In the context of 1483, for example, it is contradicted by Dominic Mancini's eyewitness report: 'I saw men burst into tears when mention was made of him [Edward V] after his removal from men's sight and when there was already suspicion that he had been done away with.' Whatever Mancini's linguistic abilities or lack of them, he could understand the language of tears well enough. Ruthlessly removing political opponents, people old enough to be responsible for their own actions, was one thing; killing children quite another. Even in politics children were innocent and rulers who ordered the killing of innocents inevitably found themselves likened to King Herod. Sensible rulers did not lay themselves open to this charge. It is noticeable, for example, that Henry Tudor kept the Earl of Warwick in prison from 1485 to 1499, he did not order his judicial murder until he was twenty-four years old. Equally striking is his treatment of Lambert Simnel. In 1487, Simnel was only ten years old and, though other rebels were executed, the child's life was spared. According to Polydore Vergil, it was 'because the innocent boy was too young to have given offence'. Rulers who flouted this deeply held moral commonplace paid a heavy price. In 1202, King John's removal of his child nephew Arthur led to the rapid defection of the aristocracy of Anjou and Normandy and thus to the collapse of the Angevin Empire. Similarly, in the view of the author of the Crowland *Chronicle*, it was for what Richard was believed to have done to his nephews in 1483 that he was defeated in 1485: 'In this battle it was above all else the cause of those two boys, the sons of Edward IV, which was avenged.'

Modern historians, of course, are not bound to share the opinions of contemporary chroniclers and on this issue Charles Ross certainly did not. 'It was,' he wrote, 'Richard's mistakes upon the battlefield of Bosworth, rather than any supposed guilt in the death of his nephews, which was ultimately to cost him his throne.' But did Richard make mistakes at Bosworth? Or was his cause undermined, in Michael Jones's words, by treachery and betrayal? It is in this context that Colin Richmond's suggestion, first made in 1985, that the most serious fighting actually took place not at the traditional battlefield site but

BOSWORTH OR DADLINGTON?

THIS MAP IS BASED ON that in Charles Ross, *Richard III*. He used it to support his contention that the outcome of the battle was decisively shaped by

> the physical confines of Ambien Hill ... Hence Richard's army was in column, one battle behind the next. Only Norfolk's vanguard was directly involved in heavy fighting ... Northumberland's rearguard was never seriously engaged, nor could be, whatever the proclivities of its commander.

However, ever since Colin Richmond's 'The Battle of Bosworth', it has seemed increasingly likely that the battle was fought much nearer Dadlington and Crown Hill, probably near the line of the old Roman road along which Henry Tudor had been advancing. On the map below, the black triangles are the forces of Henry Tudor and the white ones Richard III.

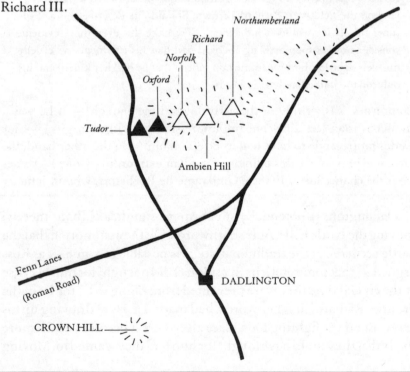

RICHARD III'S INTERNATIONAL REPUTATION

IN VIEW OF the significant foreign contribution to the overthrow of Richard III, his reputation in the eyes of foreign observers becomes a matter of some importance. One of the shrewdest commentators on the European political scene, Philippe de Commynes was in no doubt:

> The duke had his two nephews murdered and himself made king, with the title King Richard. The two daughters [of Edward IV] were declared illegitimate in a plenary session of parliament and their right to the royal arms was taken away from them. All his late brother's servants, or at least those he could capture, were killed on his orders. The cruelty did not last long; for after he had become more filled with pride than any of his predecessors as kings of England in the last hundred years and he had killed the duke of Buckingham and gathered a large army, God raised up an enemy against him who had no power ... A battle was fought. King Richard was killed and the earl of Richmond was crowned king of England on the field with Richard's crown. Should one describe this as Fortune? Surely it was God's judgement. To make this even more evident, consider how as soon as King Richard had had his two nephews cruelly murdered, he lost his wife (some said indeed that he had her killed) and his only son too immediately afterwards.

Commynes was writing in the early 1490s, time enough — if he was a credulous man (certainly not the impression he wishes to give) — for Tudor propaganda to have had its effect on him. On the other hand, the earliest expression of this opinion — and an extraordinary one — comes from the chancellor of France, Guillaume de Rochefort, who in January

at Dadlington, is potentially much more significant than 'merely' moving the battle half a mile southwards. On the assumption that the battle occurred at the traditional site, it is possible to argue — as Ross argued — that some of Richard's soldiers did not fight for him because at the crucial time they were prevented from doing so by the lie of the ground; Richard, in other words, had made a mess of drawing up his army. But if the fighting took place elsewhere it becomes much more likely that they could have fought for him had they wanted to. Moving

1484, in the course of an address to the States-General assembled at Tours, said, 'see what has happened in England since the death of King Edward. His children, already big and courageous, have been slaughtered with impunity, and their murderer, with the support of the people, has received the crown.'

The view of the French government might well be thought to be politically motivated and therefore highly suspect, but it is not so easy to see why Ferdinand of Aragon and Isabella of Castile should have held similarly biased views as early as 1485–6. Yet a letter written on 1 March 1486 by Mosen Diego de Valera begins by assuming that that is precisely what they thought: 'It is sufficiently well-known to your royal majesty that this Richard killed two innocent nephews of his to whom the realm belonged after his brother's life.'

The Burgundian court generally preferred to take the opposite political view from that of France, yet the Burgundian court chronicler, Jean Molinet, was equally adamant that Richard had ordered the murder of his nephews and was responsible for killing many others.

Even at the other end of the Hanseatic trade routes, in a contemporary chronicle written by a citizen of Danzig, Caspar Weinreich, the entry for 1483 includes the following: 'After Easter King Edward died in England. Later this summer Richard the king's brother seized power and had his brother's children killed and the queen secretly put away.' Then, under 1485: 'In the year 85 in the summer King Richard of England, who had had his brother's children killed, was himself killed about St Laurence's day.'

Whatever the truth of the matter, such unanimity of international opinion is striking.

the battle to Dadlington enables us to take much more seriously John Rous's dramatic picture of Richard's last moments: 'He bore himself like a noble soldier . . . honourably defended himself to his last breath, shouting again and again that he was betrayed and crying "Treason! Treason! Treason!".' If he was betrayed, then the question that has to be answered is why? Why were so few men prepared to fight for him? The question is all the more pressing in the light of Alexander Grant's analysis of Richard's foreign policy. For if Bosworth/Dadlington was

17

in effect the last battle of the Hundred Years War, then why were so few Englishmen prepared to fight against an invading army composed largely of England's traditional enemies, the French and the Scots?

Not that 1485 marked the end of the so-called Hundred Years War. Henry VIII, hoping to emulate Henry V, was to reopen that ancient conflict (though the skirmish at Guinegate in 1513 hardly qualifies as a battle). None the less, what Grant shows is that in the history of Anglo-French relations 1485 has a hitherto unsuspected significance. Richard was removed, not only because he was a dangerously destabilizing force in domestic politics, but also because he was a dangerously destabilizing force in international affairs (*see box on pages 16–17*).

In the end, the central fact is this: Richard was removed, and removed swiftly. The institution of monarchy may have been thrown into crisis — but it was a short-lived crisis. This, I suggest, demonstrates the underlying strength and resilience of the monarchy at this date. In the English *regnum politicum et regale* it did not require a revolution to unseat a king. It was possible for an unsatisfactory adult ruler to be ousted and replaced by someone more acceptable without society at large being turned upside down. In this sense, there were some rebellions which helped to preserve the institution of monarchy, and in England they did so at relatively little cost to the general population. It was this which led the contemporary French political commentator, Philippe de Commynes, to a striking judgement:

> Now in my opinion out of all the countries which I have personally known, England is the one where public affairs are best conducted and regulated with least violence to the people. Neither the countryside nor the people are destroyed nor are buildings burnt or demolished. Misfortune falls only on soldiers and on nobles.

Moreover, the removal of an unacceptable king did not take long. Richard III's fate was very similar to that of Richard II. In 1397 Richard II began to act in a way which led to him being widely regarded as tyrannical; in 1399 he was overthrown. In this sense he, like Richard III, lasted just two years. The most significant feature of Richard III's reign is its brevity.

FURTHER READING

In order to place Richard's reign in the context of English kingship see John Cannon and Ralph Griffiths, *The Oxford Illustrated History of the British Monarchy* (Oxford, 1988). To place it in the context of the civil wars of the fifteenth century, begin with a concise introduction, A. J. Pollard, *The Wars of the Roses* (London, 1988); also John Gillingham, *The Wars of the Roses* (London, 1981).

On individual kings see C. D. Ross, *Edward IV* (London, 1974); Rosemary Horrox, *Richard III: A Study of Service* (Cambridge, 1989); A. J. Pollard, *Richard III and the Princes in the Tower* (Gloucester, 1991) which is splendidly illustrated; and A. Grant, *Henry VII* (London, 1986).

Particularly useful are books which largely consist of extracts from primary sources, e.g. J. R. Lander, *The Wars of the Roses* (Gloucester, 1990); K. Dockray, *Richard III. A Reader in History* (Gloucester, 1988); and P. W. Hammond and Anne F. Sutton, *Richard III: The Road to Bosworth Field* (London, 1985).

Thanks to Penguin Classics, one fifteenth-century politician whose views are readily accessible is Philippe de Commynes, *Memoirs*, trans. Michael Jones (Harmondsworth, 1972). The transcript of the television trial is both revealing and entertaining, R. Drewett and M. Redhead, *The Trial of Richard III* (Gloucester, 1984).

On Bosworth and the place of 1485 as a turning-point in English history see Michael Bennett, *The Battle of Bosworth* (Gloucester, 1985). Unluckily, Bennett's book appeared just too early to be able to take account of Colin Richmond's 'The Battle of Bosworth', *History Today* (August 1985). The debate which this article provoked has been carried on very largely in the pages of *The Ricardian* which is published quarterly by the Richard III Society. Indeed, a highly cost-effective way of keeping up with the literature on later fifteenth-century history is to join this society (current annual subscription £9).

Chapter II

RICHARD, DUKE OF GLOUCESTER: THE FORMATIVE YEARS

Michael Hicks

THE FUTURE RICHARD III was born into the House of York, one of the greatest of English noble families. His father and namesake, Richard Duke of York, was the most important nobleman in England, Wales and Ireland. His mother, the Duchess Cecily, one of the prolific Neville clan, made Richard cousin to almost the whole peerage. Their pedigrees descended through three lines from Edward III and in 1460 Duke Richard was recognized by Parliament as rightful heir of the crown of England. Young Richard owed much to his splendid lineage.

At first, however, he was that most insignificant of beings, a younger son. He was the seventh child and fourth son of the duke to reach maturity. Young sons of even the highest nobility could hope only for marriage to a wealthy heiress or promotion in the Church if they were to maintain the aristocratic lifestyle to which they were accustomed. Young Richard and his slightly older brother George were literally of no account. If Duke Richard made plans for his younger sons, we cannot know what they were, for he died in battle at Wakefield in 1460, as did his second son, Edmund. When the duke's eldest son succeeded as King Edward IV in 1461, his two younger sons — George and Richard — became royal princes, next in line to the throne and crucial allies to the new king. Edward created George Duke of Clarence and Richard Duke of Gloucester. At first they continued their education; then at sixteen each embarked on a hectic

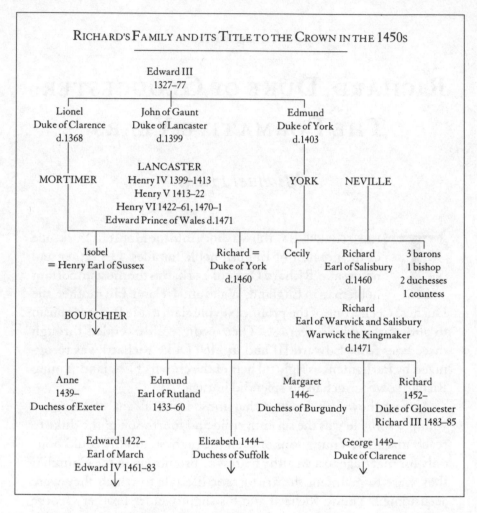

RICHARD'S FAMILY AND ITS TITLE TO THE CROWN IN THE 1450s

Edward III
1327–77

Lionel	John of Gaunt	Edmund
Duke of Clarence	Duke of Lancaster	Duke of York
d.1368	d.1399	d.1403

MORTIMER

LANCASTER
Henry IV 1399–1413
Henry V 1413–22
Henry VI 1422–61, 1470–1
Edward Prince of Wales d.1471

YORK   NEVILLE

Isobel
= Henry Earl of Sussex

Richard =   Cecily   Richard   3 barons
Duke of York   Earl of Salisbury 1 bishop
d.1460   d.1460   2 duchesses
                                    1 countess

BOURCHIER

Richard
Earl of Warwick and Salisbury
Warwick the Kingmaker
d.1471

Anne	Edmund	Margaret	Richard
1439–	Earl of Rutland	1446–	1452–
Duchess of Exeter	1433–60	Duchess of Burgundy	Duke of Gloucester
			Richard III 1483–85

Edward 1422–   Elizabeth 1444–   George 1449–
Earl of March   Duchess of Suffolk   Duke of Clarence
Edward IV 1461–83

political career; and at thirty-two Richard, by then last survivor of the brothers, was a hardened veteran of long and varied experience.

Almost nothing is known of Richard's early years. Until 1459, when he was seven, we know only the bare fact of his birth at Fotheringhay in Northamptonshire on 2 October 1452. The tales of his unnatural birth and deformity originate only after his death. Since Richard's elder brothers had a separate establishment, it seems likely that Richard and his younger siblings lived with their mother, perhaps principally at Fotheringhay and Ludlow. It was at Ludlow, the centre of York's Welsh estates, that George, Richard and their mother were captured by Henry VI's government in 1459.

Some rapid reversals of fortune then followed, ending in 1461 when George and Richard were able to join their brother Edward IV and share in the celebration of his triumphant accession. Now knights and royal dukes, George and Richard lived mostly at Greenwich Palace until about 1464. Richard was still there in May 1465, when the palace was given to Edward IV's new queen, but by September that year he had been placed in the household of the Earl of Warwick: a conventional way of preparing for his future life by learning from example. His sojourn in Warwick the Kingmakers's household *could* (and, perhaps, *ought* to) have been one of the most formative periods of his life, but scarcely anything is known about it. At least once, Richard visited the church of St Mary's Warwick with his host; he was at York in 1465 and thereabouts in 1468–9, but whether he visited Warwick's northern or Welsh castles must be mere surmise. Finally, late in 1468, when he was sixteen years old, Richard was adjudged mature enough to start his own career.

Late medieval noblemen needed to be proficient with the weapons of a soldier, the manners of a courtier, the literacy of an administrator and the habit of command of a ruler. These were the qualities that Richard's upbringing sought to instil and which were put to extreme test over the three years 1468–71.

Richard's initiation into adult politics was dramatic. It began quietly enough, when he acted as a justice in a treason trial and went on progress with the king in East Anglia. In July 1469, however, a *coup d'état* was staged by Warwick and Richard's brother Clarence, who overthrew three of Edward's most trusted earls, took over the government themselves and imprisoned the king. Richard rallied to Edward on his release and attended the autumn Great Council, which reshuffled and strengthened the regime. He remained loyal in 1470 when Warwick and Clarence rebelled again; and in the autumn of that year, when Edward was driven into exile, Richard went with him. Returning in 1471, Richard fought in the battles of Barnet and Tewkesbury, where Warwick and the Lancastrians were defeated, and shared in Edward's restoration to his crown. He had stood the test. His good service had confirmed his value to Edward suggested by his birth. Fresh opportunities beckoned. The years 1471–83 constitute a distinct and highly successful phase in Richard's ducal career.

Richard now stood at the very apex of society. Born into the aristocracy, he was not just a knight but one of the twenty-four knights of the Garter; not just a peer but one of the six dukes; and, moreover, one of the princes and brothers of the king. This was a time when the royal family was being set apart and above other men. In 1483, Parliament authorized the royal family to wear especially splendid clothes forbidden to ordinary dukes. Richard accumulated an unprecedented clutch of the prestigious honorary offices of State: Admiral of England, Great Chamberlain of England in succession to Warwick and Clarence, and Constable of England, the post that the queen's brother, Earl Rivers, coveted. Richard was thus one of the inner circle of aristocrats most closely identified with the king, the court and the government.

The contemporary Italian historian Mancini wrongly declared that Richard was seldom at court. Our patchy records frequently reveal his activities on the national scene. He swore an oath of allegiance to Prince Edward (the future Edward V) in 1471, accompanied the king on his invasion of France in 1475, participated in the ceremonial reburial of his father at Fotheringhay in 1476 and in the wedding of King Edward's younger son Richard in 1478. He attended each of Edward's parliaments in 1472–5, 1478 and 1483, appeared irregularly in council and was to be seen occasionally in London or in the king's company.

The nobility did not just take precedence over their social inferiors, they also wielded authority over them. They were lords to their households, tenants and retainers, who owed obedience to their commands. Their authority was supplemented by local office, such as the royal commissions of the peace and musters and the special judicial tribunals to which Richard was appointed. Additionally, as admiral, he had not only naval duties but also responsibilities for the administration of international maritime law. His court adjudicated lawsuits relating to trade, piracy and prizes. Richard's commands and decisions in Somerset and Dorset were authenticated by a surviving seal; presumably he had others for other counties. Similarly, as Constable of England, Richard had responsibilities not just in wartime but also for the conduct of jousts; indeed he revised the regulations for tournaments. We may presume that he possessed a seal as constable and perhaps yet another as great chamberlain. Others probably existed for him as Warden of the West Marches, Sheriff of Cumberland, Keeper of the Northern Forests and Chief Steward of the Duchy of Lancaster, all capacities in which he exercised authority. Those aggrieved with his decisions in these various capacities could appeal to the king, but in certain lordships he had authority like that of the king (regalian rights), the king himself having none, he was in effect the king. This was true of his Welsh marcher lordship of Glamorgan, the seal of which hangs from one of his charters, of his other Welsh lordships of Abergavenny, Pains Castle, Elfael and Ogmore. From 1483 he should have had another for his new regalian county (county palatine) of Cumberland.

Of course Richard did not always (or, perhaps, ever) act in these capacities himself. He delegated matters to his staff, to an expert civil lawyer in admiralty matters and to a Cumbrian gentleman as under-sheriff in Cumberland. He took advice from judges, heralds and many others. He could afford to hire the best. A host of professionals managed his secretariat, his finances, estate administration and council. They handled routine matters, advised him and implemented his wishes. We possess accounts, a cartulary (book of deeds) and charters that they prepared. His finger was on the pulse, he could intervene if he wished and could initiate much informal business under his own signature or the signet ring controlled by his secretary John Kendall. An efficient administration to cope with detail and routine

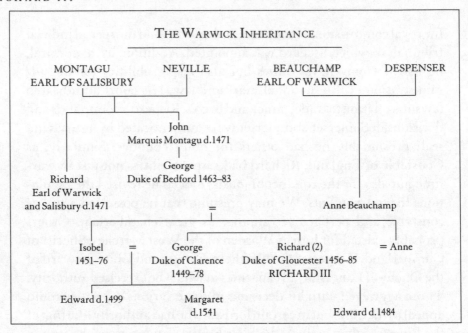

THE WARWICK INHERITANCE

MONTAGU
EARL OF SALISBURY

NEVILLE

BEAUCHAMP
EARL OF WARWICK

DESPENSER

John
Marquis Montagu d.1471

George
Duke of Bedford 1463–83

Richard
Earl of Warwick
and Salisbury d.1471

=

Anne Beauchamp

Isobel
1451–76

=

George
Duke of Clarence
1449–78

Richard (2)
Duke of Gloucester 1456–85
RICHARD III

= Anne

Edward d.1499

Margaret
d.1541

Edward d.1484

gave noblemen the leisure for a life of idle pleasure. In Richard's case, it freed him to concentrate his attention where he wished.

● ● ● ● ●

In the years after 1471, it is clear that Richard's priority was to build up a great estate capable of supporting the scale of expenditure, political and military activity that he wished to achieve. Those whom Edward had defeated in 1470–1 were regarded as traitors whose lands were confiscated and most of whose possessions were granted to Duke Richard. A grant by itself, however, was seldom enough, for the losers knew better what they had lost than Richard knew what he had gained and a host of widows, children, other relatives and dependants, trustees, creditors and retainers asserted their claims. Richard had to fight hard to make his title good and often had to compromise. Indeed, had he pursued every claim, he would have bankrupted himself in litigation and would have acquired an unmanageable estate scattered throughout England. The shape of his eventual estate was planned.

The most important element in all this was the Warwick

1 *Richard III's admiralty seal.*

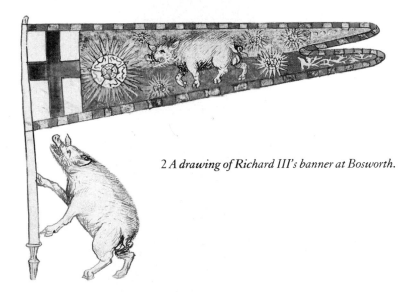

2 *A drawing of Richard III's banner at Bosworth.*

3 *Richard III's boar emblem.*

4 *Dr John Argentine, physician to Edward V and informant to Dominic Mancini.*

5 *Edward IV, Richard III's elder brother.*

*6 Portrait of Elizabeth Woodville, the wife of Edward IV
and mother of Edward V.*

7 A triptych of the Wydeville marriage as legitimate.

Inheritance. Like all the greatest noble estates, it had been built up over many generations by a process of inheritance, as heirs and heiresses gradually accumulated the possessions of families that had died out. Warwick the Kingmaker himself was heir of the Nevilles through his father and heir of the Montagu earls of Salisbury through his mother. His countess was heiress of her father Richard Beauchamp, Earl of Warwick and of her mother Isobel Despenser. Warwick the Kingmaker was not only the greatest nobleman, but also the greatest traitor of his day. His estate was the most attractive of forfeitures. Since, however, his elder daughter Isobel was married to Clarence, whose change of sides in 1471 had materially contributed to King Edward's restoration, this was an estate which could not be confiscated and Isobel and Clarence were allowed to inherit it. With one exception. One element of Warwick's possessions, the Neville part, was entailed in the male line and could be inherited only by a male Neville. Isobel could never have had it. The rightful claimant was George, son of another traitor, Warwick's brother John. Edward therefore felt free to give the Neville lands to Richard.

Richard was dissatisfied and wanted more. He therefore sought out and married Warwick's younger daughter, Anne Neville, apparently in 1472–4, and demanded her half-share of the Warwick Inheritance from Clarence. Actually Richard meant to have more than half. Clarence refused, perhaps understandably, and the brothers quarrelled bitterly and threatened public order. Early in 1472, they argued their cases before the king's council and Edward IV decided in principle on a division. This had still not taken place in mid-1473, when they came close to private war in the Midlands, but in 1474–5 the king enforced a partition in Parliament that was just to both men, but clearly satisfied neither. The whole Warwick Inheritance, including the Neville lands, was divided on a geographical basis, Richard receiving the lands in Wales and the North and Clarence those in the Midlands. Ill-will persisted and when Clarence fell in 1477–8 Richard was quick to improve on his share.

The dispute over the Warwick Inheritance is representative of

DEMANDING MONEY WITH MENACES: RICHARD DUKE OF GLOUCESTER AND ELIZABETH COUNTESS OF OXFORD

MOST DEFEATED LANCASTRIANS submitted to Edward IV in 1471, but not the Earl of Oxford, who fought on until 1474. Naturally, the king denied all help to the traitor and thus, as usual in such cases, he had Oxford's relatives interned. The earl's mother, the Dowager-Countess Elizabeth, was placed in the 'keeping and the rule' (custody) of Richard Duke of Gloucester, who around Christmas 1472 arrested her at the nunnery of Stratford le Bow (Essex), seized her keys and coffers, and imprisoned her in a house at Stepney.

Harsh though her treatment might appear, thus far it was probably normal, but Gloucester exploited the situation to his personal advantage. Already the recipient of the earl's confiscated lands, he also coveted those of the countess, who had appointed trustees to hold them after her death. Old and sick, Elizabeth was easy to coerce and so were her trustees. While one was summoned to 'speak with her *if he dared*' and another was brow-beaten as a 'false priest and hypocrite', both urged her fearfully to give in, which she did, thankful that her lands could be used as a bargain for better treatment. Having yielded, she was allowed to move to more

several other rivalries. Richard's vigour and aggression repeatedly brought success. He exploited the king's favour and authority to the full. He and Clarence had overridden the rights of Warwick's countess and George Neville, both still alive, but helpless in the face of the king's wishes. Richard took similar advantage of the aged Countess of Oxford and Lady Hungerford to secure their inheritances. As royal dukes, he and Clarence commanded authority shared by few others and they could get away with conduct that the king would tolerate in nobody else. Only thus could those without inheritances of their own establish great estates.

● ● ● ● ●

When suitors presented their books to King Edward, birth, rank, title and connections placed Richard among those courtiers behind the throne who were depicted in illuminations. He could whisper in the pleasant accommodation at Walbrook. The first deed conveying her lands to Gloucester had to be forged, because some trustees had resisted and gone into hiding, but the duke sued them in the courts. He won his case, though not until the unfortunate countess had died and could no longer deny his false claim that he had bought her lands. Later he gave many of her lands to his new college at Middleham.

Eyewitnesses recalled how the countess wept and lamented at her arrest, how she cried repeatedly as the duke pressurized her, and how bitterly she regretted her surrender, both at the time and afterwards. Wholly in the duke's power, her Achilles heel was her fear of the North, which Gloucester exploited ruthlessly. Terrified 'that he would send her to Middleham, considering her great age, the great journey, and the great cold which then was of frost and snow, fearing that she could not ensure to be conveyed thither without great jeopardy of her life, and also sore fearing how she would be treated' on arrival, Elizabeth gave in. Frivolous though they may at first appear, her fears were justified by her death within the year. Gloucester's strong-arm tactics were condemned, not only by Elizabeth's allies, but also by King Edward, the Lord Chancellor and even his own retainers, but none dared to intervene. Gloucester himself acted without pity or scruple.

king's ear, share in his decisions and press in person for favours. Status and influence commanded respect, but should not be equated with power or fortune. They counted for little in times of crisis and civil war. Kings shared power because it was the aristocracy who possessed the brute force to make their wills prevail. They were a *landed aristocracy*. Ultimately it was their lands, not their rank or titles that mattered.

Warwick the Kingmaker had been the greatest of such men and Richard wished to emulate him. He built on Warwick's ruins. It was as conqueror that in 1471 he secured the Neville lordships of Middleham and Sheriff Hutton in Yorkshire and Penrith in Cumberland. But the marriage to Anne Neville that brought him Barnard Castle also meant that henceforth he received the loyalty as well as the obedience of Warwick's men. He was a resident lord, who spent his

The Treaty that made Richard the Lord of the North

THIS INDENTURE made the 28th day of July the 14th year of the reign of our sovereign lord King Edward IV between the right high and mighty prince Richard Duke of Gloucester on the one part and the right worshipful lord Henry Earl of Northumberland on the other part witnesses:

1. That the said Earl by this present letter promises and grants unto the said Duke to be his faithful servant, the said Duke being his good and faithful lord. And the said Earl promises to do service to the said Duke at all times lawful and convenient when he thereunto by the said Duke shall be lawfully required, the duty of the allegiance of the said Earl to the king's highness, the queen, his service and promise to Prince Edward their first begotten son, and all the king's issue begotten and to be begotten, first at all times reserve and had.

southern revenues in the North on buildings, local monasteries and on generous fees to any retainers. Fees absorbed almost all his income from Middleham as he recruited most of the gentry of Richmondshire, where he was unchallengeable as were Henry Percy, Earl of Northumberland, and Ralph Neville, Earl of Westmorland, 'rulers' respectively of Northumberland and County Durham. We cannot recapture the splendour of his life, even at Middleham Castle where the upper storeys of the castle built by Richard have disappeared, but his military might is easily glimpsed in the high towers and walls of Castle Barnard across the Tees or Richmond above the River Swale.

Even in the North, Warwick had been more than a leading lord and Richard too had high aspirations. He exploited his influence with King Edward to secure whatever other lordships and offices he had to give. The list is most impressive. He courted the city of York, recruited retainers even from beyond his lands in Northumberland, County Durham and eastern Yorkshire, and boldly confronted

2. For the which service the said Duke promises and grants unto the said Earl to be his good and faithful lord at all times and to sustain him in his right before all other persons, except those excluded above. Also the said Duke promises and grants to the said Earl that he shall not ask, challenge, nor claim any office or offices or fee that the said Earl has of the king's grant or of any other person or persons at the making of these present letters, nor interrupt the said Earl nor any of his servants in executing or doing of any of the said office or offices by him or any of his servants in time to come.

3. And also the said Duke shall not accept nor retain into his service any servant or servants that was or any time since has been retained by the said Earl of fee, clothing or promise. According to the agreement made between the said Duke and Earl by the king's highness and the lords of his council at Nottingham the 12th day of May in the 13th year of the reign of our sovereign lord, John Wedrington only except.

In witness whereof the said Duke and the said Earl to these indentures interchangeably have set their seals the day and year abovesaid.

the other northern lords in their home territories. They were challenged to accept his mastery or resort to private war. By retaining John Wedrington, the undersheriff used to rule Northumberland by the Percy earl, Richard trespassed on his essential interests and prompted an appeal to the king. Fearful of civil war, king and council restored the status quo and decreed on 12 June 1473 that Richard must not retain the earl's men.

Richard could have remained merely a northern lord rather than *the* 'Lord of the North'. Here the records fail us. We cannot know precisely what followed: what charm, persuasions, blandishment and inducements Richard offered. What we do know is that little more than a year later, on 28 July 1474, the duke and earl sealed an agreement whereby the Percy earl submitted to Richard's lordship and Richard promised his favour to the earl. In practice, Richard left Northumberland and the East Riding to the earl and the earl allowed Richard a free hand elsewhere in Yorkshire and west of the Pennines. But it was

GLOUCESTER'S PROGRESS TO BE 'LORD OF THE NORTH' 1470–83

YEAR	ACQUISITION OF LANDS AND PROPERTY	PROMOTION TO OFFICES
1470		Warden of West March
1471	Lordships of Middleham, Sheriff Hutton and Penrith	Chief Steward of Duchy of Lancaster in North for life
1472	Custodies of property in Cumberland	Keeper of forests beyond Trent for life Steward of Ripon
1473		
1474	Lordship of Barnard Castle Town of Scarborough	
1475	Lordship of Skipton-in-Craven	Sheriff of Cumberland for life
1476		
1477		
1478	Lordships of Richmond and of Helmsley	
1479		
1480		
1481		
1482		Lieutenant-General of the North
1483	County Palatine of Cumberland	Hereditary Warden of West March

more than a defensive compromise. The two men worked together in Yorkshire, arbitrating disputes between retainers, clearing fishgarths that impeded navigation and indulging in mining speculations. The earl gave good service and Richard trusted him. There was warmth in their relationship which made it work and their treaty was a model for the other lords. All the other northern peers, even the Earl of Westmorland, accepted Richard's supremacy and became his men. Through them and their retainers Richard became, in Professor Kendall's words, 'Lord of the North'. He used the northerners most conspicuously in 1482–3 against the Scots.

Although King Edward had not always favoured Richard's dominance in the region, once achieved he accepted it and indeed took advantage of it. The king wanted to maintain law and order — hence his veto of Richard's recruitment of Percy retainers — and defend the

Scottish borders. Like Warwick before him, Richard was King's Warden of the West Marches, responsible for the defence of Cumbria; Northumberland followed his ancestors as Warden of the East and Middle Marches. While Richard employed permanent deputies, Lord Dacre as his lieutenant and Richard Salkeld in Carlisle, he visited the borders himself and spent money on improvements to Carlisle Castle. After the outbreak of war in 1480, Richard raided Scotland the next year and in 1482 commanded a major invasion that reached Edinburgh and took Berwick. Northumberland, Neville, Earl Rivers and Lord Stanley served under his command. Twenty northerners were created knights banneret by Richard outside Berwick. Parliament congratulated him in 1483, gave him Cumberland as a palatine county independent of the king, together with whatever he could conquer in Scotland, and appointed him hereditary Warden of the West Marches. If Richard could no longer rely on royal support to defend the West March, he could keep whatever he could seize. The mission beckoning to him and his northerners was the conquest of south-western Scotland, instead when Richard became king they were his most dependable agents for the rule of southern England.

●   ●   ●   ●   ●

Richard's place in society was determined by his birth, his rank, his fortune and his lineage. Even at birth, he was a member of the House of York. He had his place on the family tree and was entitled to use his father's coat of arms, distinguished by a label to indicate his *cadet* or junior status. His brother's accession entitled him to use the royal arms, again differenced with a label of three points. Following his creation as knight of the Garter in 1465, an enamel plate bearing his arms was affixed to the rear of his stall in St George's Chapel, Windsor, probably in 1466. The crest atop his helm was a lion collared with a label with three points and his shield bore the royal arms — the three lions of England and three fleurs-de-lis of France — differenced by a label of three points. So, too, his seal as lord admiral portrayed his flagship with sails depicting the royal arms with a difference and flying a banner with the same emblem. Anybody proficient in heraldry could

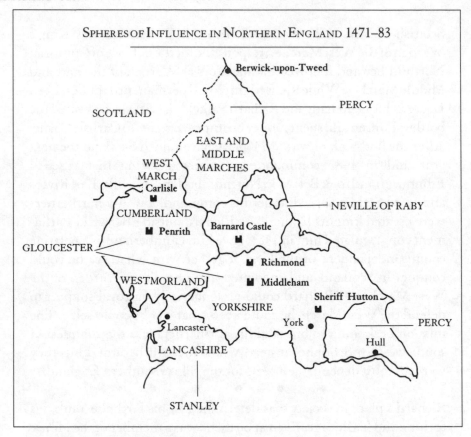

SPHERES OF INFLUENCE IN NORTHERN ENGLAND 1471–83

Berwick-upon-Tweed

PERCY

SCOTLAND

EAST AND
MIDDLE
MARCHES

WEST
MARCH
Carlisle

CUMBERLAND

NEVILLE OF RABY

Penrith

Barnard Castle

GLOUCESTER

Richmond

WESTMORLAND

Middleham

Sheriff Hutton

YORKSHIRE

Lancaster

York

PERCY

Hull

LANCASHIRE

STANLEY

identify Garter plate, banner or shield as Richard's and recognize the subtle difference from those of Clarence.

Richard's position was defined more precisely and made more distinctively his own by his marriage to Anne Neville. To his original membership of the House of York and his status as a royal prince, he added his role as heir of the Beauchamp earls of Warwick in the *Rous Roll* and *Beauchamp Pageant*, as heir of the Montagus in the *Salisbury Roll* and as heir of the Despensers in the Tewkesbury Abbey *Chronicle*. In each case, Richard's royal arms are quartered with his wife's much more complex coat recording all the noble families from which she sprang. Richard enshrined a whole range of families, estates, loyalties and traditions. His cartulary recorded the rights, privileges and un-

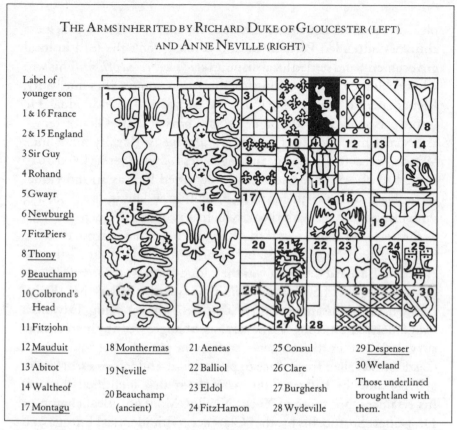

THE ARMS INHERITED BY RICHARD DUKE OF GLOUCESTER (LEFT) AND ANNE NEVILLE (RIGHT)

Label of younger son

1 & 16 France
2 & 15 England
3 Sir Guy
4 Rohand
5 Gwayr
6 Newburgh
7 FitzPiers
8 Thony
9 Beauchamp
10 Colbrond's Head
11 Fitzjohn

12 Mauduit	18 Monthermas	21 Aeneas	25 Consul	29 Despenser
13 Abitot	19 Neville	22 Balliol	26 Clare	30 Weland
14 Waltheof	20 Beauchamp (ancient)	23 Eldol	27 Burghersh	Those underlined brought land with them.
17 Montagu		24 FitzHamon	28 Wydeville	

satisfied claims that he had inherited from each. Quite properly as heir of the Nevilles, he founded a fair at Middleham and, once king, was nevertheless expected to favour Warwick as heir of the Beauchamps. The other side of the coin was that he could call on loyalties due to all these families. To divorce or poison his wife, as he was later accused, imperilled them all.

Richard fulfilled contemporary expectations as member of the houses of York, Neville, Montagu, Beauchamp and Despenser. He lived the noble life of conspicuous consumption appropriate to his rank: he dressed richly; resided in stone castles surrounded by a large household of liveried retainers; ate and drank expensively; attended several religious services a day; read histories and romances for

35

pleasure; commissioned extensions to his castles and new collegiate churches; attended Parliament and council; took the lead in local government; and settled local disputes *as was expected of him*. This was what noblemen did, according to convention, some well, some badly, Richard perhaps better than most. But he was also an individual. He wrote personal letters and signed them himself — R. Gloucester — and sometimes added his motto, *loyaulté me lie* (loyalty binds me). Whatever it actually meant, and regardless of whether he lived up to it, he had chosen it himself and it identified him as an individual separable from his birth, his rank, his family and his in-laws. So, too, with his badge of the white boar, which he preferred to such emblems as the bear-and-ragged-staff that he could have chosen from those he had inherited. Stone boars stamp as his work parts of the castle and church at Barnard Castle. It was the badge that was recorded against his name in Writhe's *Garter Roll*. This was the badge that distinguished the thousand retainers that he took on King Edward's expedition to France in 1475. Several such badges worn by his retainers survive. Whether Richard sat in state in the great hall of Middleham Castle or travelled from place to place, his attendants or escort wore a livery and the badge of the white boar that identified them as his retainers, not those of York, Neville, Montagu, Beauchamp or Despenser. So, too, his brother Clarence, with identical lineage and marriage, decked out his men in green with black bull badges. Each duke chose a separate identity for all his men. They, however, must have remembered their different origins and offered variable qualities of service.

Some noblemen were mere stereotypes; nonentities, who filled their destined role, but made no mark in their own day or on posterity. Richard's brother-in-law, John Duke of Suffolk, was as insignificant as it was possible for a duke to be. Richard, however, was no mere cipher. If his behaviour was conditioned by a multitude of expectations and he depended on a host of experts to administer what he could not handle himself, he was nevertheless the individual who made decisions on the basis of his chosen priorities, his considered judgement and his personal tastes. He alone could have decided to develop his power in the North rather than in Wales. If his piety was no more conventional and influenced by easily identifiable sources, the combination of his interest in the mystic Mechthild of Hackeborn, his cult of St Ninian and St Cuthbert, and the colleges he founded at Middleham and Barnard Castle was nevertheless unique. He was a sensual man — witness his bastards — and capable of strong passions. He could make up his own mind and had distinct preferences. It was Richard in person who argued with Clarence over the Warwick Inheritance in the royal council in 1472, who seized and threatened the Countess of Oxford, who opposed his brother's shameful Treaty of Picquigny and he who charmed the citizens of York. Complex and many-sided, he was a formidable egotist. Undoubtedly in control of his own affairs, which he extended to embrace the whole of the North, Richard's forcible interventions elsewhere were not to be ignored. Nobody should have supposed that they could determine the minority government of Edward V without his participation.

FURTHER READING

The best surveys are C. D. Ross, *Richard III* (London, 1991); A. J. Pollard, *North-Eastern England during the Wars of the Roses: Lay Society, War, and Politics 1450–1500* (Oxford, 1990); and M. A. Hicks, *Richard III as Duke of Gloucester: A Study in Character* (Borthwick Paper 70, York, 1986), which concentrates on 1471–83. Particular aspects are treated in M. A. Hicks, *Rivals of Richard III: Magnates and their Motives in Fifteenth-Century England* (Hambledon, 1991), chapters 10, 14–20, 23; essays by M. A. Hicks, A. J. Pollard and R. B. Dobson in *Kings and Nobles in the Later Middle Ages: A Tribute to Charles Ross*, ed. R. A. Griffiths and J. W. Sherborne (Gloucester, 1986); and essays by M. A. Hicks, Rosemary Horrox, Michael Jones and D. M. Palliser in *Richard III and the North*, ed. Rosemary Horrox (Hull, 1985). Some additional information is collected in Rosemary Horrox, *Richard III: A Study of Service* (Cambridge, 1989). Paul Murray Kendall, *Richard III* (London, 1955) is still worth reading.

Chapter III

1483: THE YEAR OF DECISION (OR TAKING THE THRONE)

Colin Richmond

THE USURPATION of the Crown by Richard Duke of Gloucester is a mystery. It will always remain so: Richard's motives for depriving Edward V of the throne are hidden from us and it is unlikely that new evidence (if forthcoming) will be conclusive. Indeed, it is impossible: even if persuasive new evidence were to be found, it would never be accepted as such by one or other of the embattled parties in the controversy over the character of the usurper, a controversy which has lasted nearly 400 years and currently exhibits every sign of continuing for another 400.

The passion and the commitment which are never absent from this controversy are hard to account for, save by that dogged attachment to political misjudgement, miscalculation and ultimate political failure to which the English are prone. But there are good reasons for sharp disagreement. The reasons are these: on the one hand, the usurpation is politics at their most extreme; on the other, contemporary comment is confused by such extremes. Both these points require elaboration. English kings had been disposed of before 1483, in the case of Edward II in a fairly extreme fashion. Edward II, Richard II and Henry VI, however, were fully grown men who had, over many years, shown what dangerously incompetent kings they were. Their removal was by a political community which could take no more of their disruptive behaviour. Richard of Gloucester replaced his twelve-year-old nephew before Edward had had a chance to show what sort of king he would make. Moreover, Richard also killed his nephew. Also usurpation and murder were achieved in a breathlessly short time — no more than three (or perhaps four) months. People were taken aback then; they still are today. We are confronted with political behaviour of such staggering unconventionality that if we want to explain, rather than simply gape, we must be prepared for the unpalatable. Contemporaries had to confront the unpalatable directly. It left them gaping too. This brings us to the second introductory point: contemporary confusion.

There are three contemporaries who recorded the usurpation at length. Two of these observed it (from very different standpoints) for themselves; the third was Thomas More. More was five years old in 1483; he wrote his *History of King Richard the Third* twenty years later. It was a young man's book and he gave up writing it once he had dealt with the usurpation. The *History* has been understandably influential in accounts and interpretations of the usurpation; Thomas More had a good knowledge of people and events. It is, none the less, a book that should not, indeed must not, be used by historians — except as what once used to be termed 'a jolly good read'. The *History* is the sort of work we have become much more attuned to since the arrival on our television screens of historical re-creations which meld fact and fancy into a plausible, entertaining and instructive story. More does the same. At this remove, it is impossible to discern in his *History* what *is* history. We should not attempt the impossible.

Dominic Mancini, the second of our contemporary writers, was an Italian who was in London from just before the death of Edward IV on 9 April 1483 until just after the coronation of Richard III three months later on 6 July. He wrote up the astonishing episode he had accidentally witnessed when he returned to France; he dated the piece, which is in Latin, 1 December 1483 — the English title is 'The Usurpation of Richard III'. Thus, it was written soon after the usurpation, but not immediately after. Mancini had had time to tell, more than once no doubt, his remarkable story; he must have been as eager to recount what he had seen as his listeners were to hear of the astonishing turn English politics had taken from one who had been there. We have all been in this position. We all know how the story we have to tell acquires interpretative gloss (as well as a high polish) the more we tell it. His informants (apparently folk who had been in the court of Edward IV and who after the king's death were in a kind of no man's land) certainly told him in French or Latin or Italian, a good deal of gossip about past as well as current events: this colours, probably highly colours, Mancini's reading of those events. Hence his version of the usurpation as an outsider looking in is to be used with caution.

Our third writer was very much an insider. He is the anonymous continuator of the Crowland *Chronicle*. He wrote the continuation, which covers the years between 1459 and 1486, in 1486. He devotes almost as much space to the reign of Richard III as he does to the previous twenty-four years. He does so intentionally, for his theme is the self-destruction of the House of York, and Richard's part in that tragedy (or is it a melodrama?) is by far the largest. Such a theme, particularly when composed so early, indicates a sophisticated author. Without doubt, this is what the Crowland Continuator is; and whoever he is he is a shrewd commentator. Some have suggested he was Henry Sharp, who had been Protonotary of the Chancery for twenty-two years by 1483; if not, he was someone very like him — a senior civil servant who knew the ways of Westminster and who cast a sardonic eye upon the doings of politicians. He was in a perfect position to observe the unforgettable events of 1483 and by that date had sufficient experience to judge the men who made, or in the case of Richard mis-made, them. The half a dozen pages this remarkable analyst devotes to the usurpation are as sure a guide as we are likely to get; much of what follows is based upon them.

It is helpful for an understanding of the period between Edward IV's sudden death on 9 April and Richard III's unexpected coronation on 6 July to divide it into four critical phases. These are: (1) the political scene in London immediately after Edward's death; (2) the arrest of Anthony Earl Rivers and his companions by Richard at Stony Stratford on 30 April — Richard's first coup; (3) Richard's four-week

---

TABLE OF EVENTS, APRIL–JUNE 1483

Unless otherwise stated all events occur at either London or Westminster

9 April	Death of Edward IV
By 16 April	Council fixes 4 May for coronation of Edward V
20 April	Edward's funeral at Windsor
24 April	Rivers and Edward V leave Ludlow
29 April	Rivers dines with Richard and Buckingham at Northampton
30 April	Richard and Buckingham arrest Rivers at Stony Stratford; take possession of Edward V
4 May	Richard and Buckingham enter London
10 May	Richard appointed protector. Coronation rescheduled for 22 June
13 May	Writs of summons sent for Parliament on 25 June
9 June	Four-hour council meeting
10 June	Richard gives letters and confidential instructions to Ratcliffe
11 June	Ratcliffe leaves for the North
13 June	Hastings summarily executed
16 June	The queen releases Richard of York from sanctuary
17 June	Writs postponing Parliament sent out
22 June	Sermons preached in support of Richard's title
24 June	Buckingham addresses mayor and aldermen
25 June	Rivers and others executed at Pontefract
26 June	Richard takes the throne

Protectorate between early May and early June and (4) Richard's second coup, which has its origin (I am convinced) at the four-hour council meeting on Monday 9 June and its formal and undisputed end on Thursday 26 June when Richard sat on the royal throne at Westminster and thus began to reign.

I am beginning with the most contentious phase: post-Edwardian politics in London during April. The apprehension caused by the early and completely unanticipated death of Edward IV is neatly caught in a letter by John Gigur, Warden of Tattershall College in Lincolnshire, to his patron William Wainfleet, Bishop of Winchester, written on 19 April, at the very time the funeral procession was making its slow journey from London to Windsor. John wrote: 'I beseche you to remember in what jeopardy youre College of Tateshale stondyth in at this day; for nowe oure Soveren lord the Kyng ys ded we wete [. . .] not hoo schal be oure lord nor hoo schal have the reule aboute us.' As it was in the provinces, so it was in the capital. Among the councillors as they met after Edward had died, the question in all minds was 'hoo schal have the reule aboute us'.

Their joint and agreed answer seems to have been no one individual. The former king's advisers concurred with his last will (which does not survive: was it destroyed by Richard?) that the young Edward should be crowned promptly and that there should be neither Regency nor Protectorate. Edward IV, his queen, his Woodville relatives, William Lord Hastings, and Edward's other trusted officers, household and administrative, evidently hoped that around the crowned and annointed Edward V, the eldest son and uncontested heir of the late king, would group all those, or almost all of those, who had served his father. It was a realistic hope: who would wish to undermine the Yorkist dynasty? They may have pondered the absence of Henry Duke of Buckingham from the funeral at Windsor on 20 April, and thought it a bad sign, but Buckingham had little political power and less political sense. Richard's absence may have worried them more; he, however, had much to do in the North before coming to join them in the South. They had absolutely no reason at all to believe that he would dissent from their joint decision about the coronation or be other than an actively loyal uncle to his late brother's son.

This is not to say there were not tensions in London. It was a tense time. Edward's age was particularly awkward. Twelve years old, he was neither child nor man. No one could rule for him — or not for long at any rate — because he was already a lively adolescent with a mind, and more relevantly a will, of his own, yet neither could he entirely rule by himself as that mind and that will were not fully formed. This was a genuine dilemma for the experienced politicians of the council. None the less, they planned on Edward V being a focus of loyalty and a begetter of harmony. If they had a precedent in mind, it was that of 1377 when the eleven-year-old Richard II was crowned in succession to his grandfather, Edward III. Difficulties had arisen then, but not until almost a decade had passed. For all their rivalries — and Sir John Howard may have voiced some reservations — in the end the councillors seem to have sunk their differences in the common cause of as smooth a transition as possible.

While the council met in London, Richard dispatched reassuring letters from York; the Crowland Chronicler tells us: Richard 'wrote the most pleasant letters to console the queen and promised to come to offer submission, fealty and all that was due from him to his lord and king, Edward V'. But at the same time he was planning for action of an entirely opposite sort. We now move to the second phase: Richard's attack on the council's plan.

It has to be asked: why was Richard not happy with the solution of his brother and the council? One thing must be made clear: there was no Woodville faction on the council or indeed elsewhere. The Woodvilles, that is Elizabeth the queen, her brothers Anthony Earl Rivers and Lionel Bishop of Salisbury, and her sons by her first husband, Thomas Marquess of Dorset and Sir Richard Grey, did not head an affinity which was distinct from that of the late king. Such power as they had stemmed from him; that power died with him. Of course, they were influential: as the king's family they were listened to. Anthony Earl Rivers was described by Mancini as 'a kind, serious, and just man, one tested by every vicissitude of life'; there is no cause to question what can only have been the general opinion; no doubt, therefore, Rivers's views carried weight. Because he was such a paragon, Edward IV had made him governor of the household of his eldest son in 1473. In the intervening ten years, Edward discovered no cause to remove his 'kind, serious, and just' brother-in-law from that crucial post.

Nor, it must also be stressed, had there been any hostility between the Woodvilles (the family of Edward IV's wife) and Edward's brother Richard, his sole surviving brother, after they had all acquiesced in the judicial extinction of George Duke of Clarence in 1478. Richard did not skulk in the North. He was often in London, frequently at court. There is no denying he liked the North. He did too much for men and communities there to believe otherwise; moreover, as he had chosen York minster as his burial place, Yorkshire was clearly where he was most at home. This, however, is a long remove from the currently received image of him as an anti-Woodville, anti-court, anti-soft South, hard but straight northerner. Northerners (it should be said) may be as devious as southerners, or westerners, or easterners. Richard was as hard and as devious as they come, but neither deviousness nor hardness stemmed from any geographical location. They were aspects of a complicated character, which before 1483 he had not completely revealed. The gritty pursuit of his own interest Richard had exhibited: his outrageous treatment of the widowed Countess of Oxford in the 1470s (in order to divest her of her landed property) amounted to bullying which was far more than simply distasteful. However, behaviour such as this was not uncommon among the landed classes of Yorkist England; fewer of their number were offended by Richard's devotion to self-aggrandizement than we might expect.

Political deceit was another matter. When in 1483 he thought his time had come, his masterly display of dissimulation took old political campaigners by surprise. It is difficult to imagine what discontent drove him to upset (at the very outset) their genuine attempt to do what was best for all concerned or to find an answer. One is bound to fall back on paranoia as the explanation. Richad feared for his landed estate, for his vice-regal status in the North, for his political future, for his personal safety, if Edward was crowned on 4 May. These fears were not grounded in an informed assessment of current politics; they were either rooted in Richard's insecure personality or recently planted there by the Duke of Buckingham. The duke had been in touch with

45

ANTHONY WOODVILLE, EARL RIVERS

THE FORTUNES of the Woodville family were made when Edward IV married Anthony's sister Elizabeth in 1464. Born *c*. 1440, Anthony inherited the recently (in 1466) created earldom when his father Richard Woodville died in 1469. An important patron of literature and chivalry, he was one of the most cultivated figures at the Yorkist court. According to Mancini he was

> always considered a kind, serious and just man, and one tested by every vicissitude of life. Whatever his prosperity he had injured nobody, though benefiting many: and therefore he had entrusted to him the care and direction of the king's eldest son.

According to Rous, after his execution at Pontefract a hairshirt was discovered which he had long been in the habit of wearing next to his bare flesh. The shirt was then hung before the image of the Blessed Virgin Mary at the Carmelite Friars at Doncaster.

Richard as soon as Edward IV was dead — possibly even during the week that he lay dying. Buckingham had many scores to settle with that king; desire to dismantle the Edwardian settlement so dominated his limited intelligence, he had no thought for the welfare of the political community at large. Buckingham and Richard seem an ill-assorted couple: there is no likelihood that we will be able to explain their relationship satisfactorily; we simply have to accept it.

While these two plotted to undermine the continuation of the Edwardian regime proposed by the council in London, in other words to overthrow the status quo, Anthony Earl Rivers was preparing to bring Prince Edward to London for the coronation. Edward's household was established at Ludlow, where it also functioned as a conciliar government for the Welsh borders. Rivers had probably been there throughout the period of Edward IV's last illness and death; he had not attended the funeral. News of the king's death had been slow in reaching Ludlow; it took five days — Edward IV died on 9 April and a messenger arrived at Ludlow only on 14 April. There may have been straightforward reasons for the delay; whatever they were they evidently did not include urgency — there was no Woodville scheming to effect a *fait accompli* which would exclude Richard from his proper place among councillors of the new king. That idea did not enter Woodville or other heads; it was only in Richard's. If it was. The possibility that Richard cynically invented a Woodville opposition cannot be altogether rejected; if he did, he pulled the wool over the eyes of historians more thoroughly than over those of his contemporaries. Anthony Earl Rivers certainly had not the slightest antagonism towards Richard (let alone any suspicion of the fate Richard had in store for him). As recently as 20 March 1483 Rivers had accepted Richard as an arbitrator in a dispute he was having over lands with one of his Norfolk neighbours. Now, a month later, on 24 April, he blithely set off from Ludlow to convey Edward to London with no more than the 2,000 soldiers the council had agreed should accompany him. Moreover, he took a route which would enable him to encounter Richard in Northamptonshire so that they might ride together into London, where a formal welcome from the citizens awaited them. He was in for a rude shock.

On the evening of 29 April, Rivers and Sir Richard Grey rode over to Northampton from Stony Stratford, where they had arrived with the prince, to dine with Richard; 'they were greeted with a particularly cheerful and merry face', says the Crowland Chronicler, 'and sitting at the duke's table for dinner, they passed the whole time in very pleasant conversation.' After dinner, the Duke of Buckingham also arrived. The party broke up amicable and late. The next morning, Richard and Buckingham went to Stony Stratford and promptly arrested Rivers, Grey, Sir Thomas Vaughan, chamberlain of the prince, and other members of his household, explaining to the prince that they had nipped a conspiracy against themselves in the bud. This was patently untrue. The element of surprise and presumably a stronger armed following rendered opposition impossible. So skilfully executed an outrage cannot have been concocted during the early hours of the

47

morning after Rivers had left; it can only have been planned in advance. When the queen was told of what had happened she took her second son, Richard Duke of York, into sanctuary at Westminster. There was consternation in London; the sole councillor not disconcerted was William Lord Hastings; possibly he thought the balance of power had been more correctly realigned; if so, he too was to be taught a lesson in the new Ricardian politics.

Richard, Buckingham and Edward entered London on 4 May. They publicly put on show wagon-loads of what they called Woodville arms. The public no doubt laughed up its sleeve and waited for the next move of the man who had taken the upper hand. During the following few days, Richard was named protector, the coronation was rescheduled for 22 June and the council displayed unanimity and courage in opposing Richard's demand that Rivers and Grey be executed for their conspiracy. He, none the less, confiscated all Woodville property. The first coup was complete. It appears that it was acceptable to the professional politicians and administrators at Westminster: Richard made few changes in the personnel of government (at any level). The Woodvilles had gone and that was all. Evidently many observers believed, as William Lord Hastings appears to have done, that without them an even smoother course had been set for the opening of the reign of Edward V.

The third phase — of the interval in May between Richard's two coups — may be dealt with quickly. In so far as any government during a minority can be deemed normal, this was a month of normal government. Richard and the council tackled routine and pressing problems, especially financial ones: far from leaving a vast fortune, as contemporaries thought, Edward IV had precisely £1,200. 7s. 8d. in the treasury at his death. Prince Edward was lodged in the Tower of London; his household was not tampered with further; the preparations for his crowning went on apace. There is no evidence of disharmony or even unease — Richard gave little cause for any: he did not redistribute patronage; his northern followers were not yet overrunning the South; his new appointments to government office were old hands. It was only in his remarkable generosity to the Duke of Buckingham that he might have given reason for alarm. Buckingham was granted vice-regal power in Wales and the Border Counties: there had been nothing like this before (unless it had been Richard's own virtually unlimited authority in the North); there was to be nothing like it again. Whatever future plans Richard might have, it was clear Buckingham was going to be party to them.

One plan was to extend the Protectorate beyond the coronation. This would have been a departure from previous practice; for example, when Henry VI, aged nine, had been crowned in 1429 the Protectorate of his uncle Humphrey Duke of Gloucester had come to an end; Humphrey had no formal authority thereafter. Richard did not want that for himself and the speech for the opening of Parliament on 25 June, which his chancellor, John Russell, Bishop of Lincoln, was drafting during late May or early June, was to inform the political community of the continuation of Richard's formal control of government. How many knew of this impending novelty is not clear; how many, therefore, may have been disturbed by it is unknown. Was William Lord Hastings? We have reached our fourth and final phase.

On Friday 13 June Hastings was taken out of a council meeting at the Tower and beheaded. Other councillors were arrested and imprisoned: Thomas Rotherham, the Archbishop of York, John Morton, the Bishop of Ely, Oliver King, the late king's secretary who was still active in that office, and Thomas Lord Stanley, although he was shortly released. The conspiracy story was again trotted out; Richard proclaimed that Hastings was the ringleader of a plot against him. This unimaginative repetition was believed by few then and none now. If Hastings had been plotting, he would not have been so careless as to be caught utterly off-guard at a meeting of the council. On the other hand, like Anthony Earl Rivers before him, he can have had no inkling of what Richard was going to do to him. The indecent haste with which Hastings was killed shows a lesson Richard had learned: this time he was not going to risk the council letting one of his victims

49

live; William Lord Hastings was made to die without dignity. Why then did Richard remove him (and the others)? This is a key question for an understanding of the second coup. Alas, it has innumerable answers, none of them altogether satisfactory.

It is likely that something of consequence had occured at a meeting of the council at Westminster on Monday 9 June; the session was a long one lasting from ten to two o'clock. We do not know what was debated, save that no one was said to have spoken on behalf of the queen. This is enigmatic. It may be that the matter of persuading the queen to allow her second son, Richard Duke of York, to leave sanctuary so that he might take his proper place at the coronation was raised. If that was the case, however, the report that there was no support for the queen suggests there was no opposition to whatever persuasion (and we can readily imagine its nature) was proposed by Richard. And what happened on the following two days, as well as the length of the meeting itself, does suggest that Richard met resistance to some proposition of his. On 10 and 11 June 1483, he sent letters under the signet, that is under the most confidential of the royal seals, to the city of York, the Earl of Northumberland and Ralph Lord Neville (among others no doubt), asking them to raise troops and to hurry south to put down a plot of the queen to kill him and the Duke of Buckingham. The trusty old spectre of the Woodvilles is brought out to rally his northerners to their lord's threatened side. (Still, Richard cannot have anticipated their arrival in under two weeks: once again his must have been the plotting.) Had he encountered opposition at the Monday council session, led by William Lord Hastings, to more than his desire that Richard Duke of York be taken from sanctuary, to more than a renewed demand for the execution of Rivers and Grey, to more than the scheme for an extended Protectorate? Had he dared to raise the matter of taking the Crown and been taken aback at the negative response he had met? If so, the letters of 10 and 11 June may be explained and the removal of Hastings, the *chef* of the late king's household, the engine-room of the Yorkist political establishment, may be better understood; with its head cut off, the body of the

Yorkist polity would (for a sufficient time at any rate) be unable to react.

Once he had disposed of William Lord Hastings in so atrocious a fashion and taken into custody a handful of other objectors, Richard met with no more opposition; his novel brutality shocked everyone into submission.

It may be argued, though not by me, that Richard's first coup bears a relation to the political situation in London on Edward IV's death; but few, if any, would maintain that his second coup related to the first, except in the perverted logic of Richard's mind. If one event were to be singled out as a turning point, as the moment at which Richard crossed the Rubicon, it would have to be his summary execution of William Lord Hastings on Friday 13 June. It was then that he decisively broke with the English political past, when he contemptuously threw down the gauntlet to the political establishment, when he revealed what one is tempted to call his heart of darkness. The message was as clear as that of Hitler on the Night of the Long Knives in June 1934.

As a result of this one event, government business wound down from this time and petitioners ceased to arrive at Westminster: there was no point in asking Edward V for anything if he was never to be king. Richard now proceeded to clear the way for his usurpation. On Monday 16 June, by a show of force, he prevailed upon the queen to release Richard Duke of York from sanctuary. On the same day or the next, writs were dispatched postponing the coronation and Parliament until November. On 17 or 18 June, instructions were sent North for the killing of Anthony Earl Rivers, Sir Richard Grey and Sir Thomas Vaughan: this duly took place at Pontefract Castle on 25 June. No doubt during these and the following few days Richard's claim to the throne was discussed and drafted. On Sunday 22 June, sermons announcing his claim were preached in London: the gist of them seems to have been, for there was much deliberate obfuscation and mystification, that the sons of Edward IV were illegitimate because their father had made a bigamous marriage with their mother Elizabeth Woodville. It may, however, have taken longer than a few

10 JUNE 1483

Tʜᴇ ᴛᴇxᴛ of a letter written on 10 June 1483 to the mayor and city of York, delivered by Sir Richard Ratcliffe, provides the best possible insight into the kind of language Richard was using in these critical weeks:

> The Duke of Gloucester, brother and uncle of kings, Great Chamberlain, Constable and Admiral of England.
>
> Right trusty and well-beloved, we greet you well, and as ye love the weal of us, and the weal and surety of your own selves, we heartily pray you to come unto us in London in all the diligence ye can after the sight hereof, with as many as ye can make defensibly arrayed, there to aid and assist us against the queen, her blood adherents and affinity, which hath intended and daily doth intend to murder and utterly destroy us and our cousin, the duke of Buckingham, and the old royal blood of this realm, and as it is now openly known, by their subtle and damnable ways plotted the same, and also the final destruction and disinheriting of you and all other men of property and honour, as well of the north parts as other countries that belong to us.

days to piece together that version (which probably had some element of truth in it). Therefore the claim preached on 22 June, and proclaimed again on 24 June by the Duke of Buckingham to a distinguished gathering at the London Guildhall, was of a much vaguer kind. It didn't much matter. It was clear that Richard's claim was an afterthought to his decision to usurp the Crown. This he formally did on Thursday 26 June. After receiving a petition from a delegation of lords and commons urging him to take the throne, he rode to Westminster Hall and, clad in the royal robes, sat there in the marble chair of state. From this day Richard III dated his reign.

What had happened to the princes? This has been a vexed question which has received too much attention. By the end of the summer of 1483, it was widely believed that Edward and Richard of York had been killed. It is virtually impossible that they had not been. How and when those who knew were not saying — unless Thomas More's account of their murder by Sir James Tyrell is the correct version. More's story of Richard casually commissioning murder has an authentic ring to it: at Warwick in August 1483, Richard sits in the evening on his close stool; just beyond the door, Sir James Tyrell and his brother Sir Thomas, knights of the royal household, are lying awake in bed; when Richard is finished on the stool, he tells Sir James what he wants done; the next morning, Sir James rides off to London; that night the boys are murdered. But More's version may be no more than a plausible fiction; they may have been dead already. I have suggested elsewhere that they were killed on Sunday 22 June. It may be thought unlikely that Richard disposed of Edward (and Richard) even before his reign began on 25 June, but then given Richard's proven track record of killings in June, we have to consider the possibility that in these fateful days nothing was beyond him. At any rate, Dominic Mancini reports the disappearance from sight of the two boys before he left London to return to France, which he did shortly after Richard's coronation on 6 July. Mancini continues, 'already there was a suspicion that Edward had been done away with'; that suspicion may have been strongest on the part of Edward's physician, Dr John Argentine, Mancini's informant and among the last to see his patient alive.

It was the belief that Richard had murdered his young (and innocent) nephews which turned many politically influential men against him. Some of these rebelled in October 1483. Their revolt was premature. Less than two years later at Bosworth, however, Richard's accelerating descent into tyranny resulted in an unprecedented and humiliating exhibition of disloyalty to an English king, and the Yorkist dynasty was brought to a fitting end in the Leicester mud.

Why was that finale in the Leicestershire mud so appropriate? And what was the relevance of Richard's usurpation to the failure of the Yorkists? We will answer the second question first. While Richard's motives for usurping the Crown are obscure, the consequences of his usurpation are not. Some things in the past one will never be able to understand; Richard's hatred of and vindictiveness towards the

---

ANLABY CARTULARY

THE TABLE of years in a cartulary originally compiled by Thomas An-
laby in the mid century contains some entries written in a later hand.
The entry shown here beginning *Obitus Edwardi* says (in translation):
'Edward V died on 22 June; he reigned 2 months and 8 days but was not
crowned. He was killed and nobody knows where he is buried.' Since
a few lines further down it refers to Henry VII's death and burial at
Westminster, it was presumably written after, perhaps soon after, April
1509. No other near contemporary source offers a date for Edward's death.
The question is: can we believe it? The author's other dates are generally
correct, though his arithmetic — as here — is always wrong (9 April to 22
June is not 2 months and 8 days). We do not know who the author was,
and have no way of assessing what sources of information he may have
had. Since Edward's death was clearly kept a secret, only a very few can
have known. Some contemporaries living abroad believed Edward was
murdered before Richard was crowned; others thought it was later. What
is true is that on 22 June sermons were preached alleging that Edward IV's
sons were bastards.

Woodvilles seems to me one such thing. When at Stony Stratford on
the morning of 30 April he arrested Anthony Earl Rivers and Sir
Richard Grey, Richard struck a deadly blow at the consensus politics
the council had decided to adopt as the best form of government for
the country. The council's subsequent refusal of Richard's request
for the execution of Rivers and Grey was the last manifestation of
such politics. To Richard that was unacceptable: he was terrified of a
Woodville *revanche*, and so the first coup remained for him incom-
plete. It seems, therefore, that he decided on usurpation as the way to
complete it: for him (but almost only for him) it was clear that the
second coup had to follow the first. This was a disastrous decision for
the Yorkist regime and the Yorkist dynasty. To cut out the Woodvilles
from the affinity Edward IV had created was surgery the body politic
could stand; but to remove Edward IV's sons was to drive a knife into
its heart.

FURTHER READING

John Gillingham, *The Wars of the Roses* (London, 1981), is an excellent introduction to the period and its context. Paul Murray Kendall, *Richard III* (London, 1955), is an exciting introduction to its subject for the young. C. D. Ross, *Richard III* (London, 1981), is a balanced account of an unbalanced character; chapters 4 and 5 are relevant to the usurpation. Rosemary Horrox, *Richard III: A Study of Service* (Cambridge, 1989), chapter 2, is an impeccable discussion of the usurpation.

Michael Hicks, *Richard III as Duke of Gloucester: A Study in Character* (Borthwick Paper No. 70, York, 1986); Michael Hicks, 'The Last Days of Elizabeth Countess of Oxford' *English Historical Review*, vol. CIII (1988); A. J. Pollard, 'The Tyranny of Richard III', *Journal of Medieval History*, vol. 3 (1977); Charles Moreton, 'A Local Dispute and the Politics of 1483: Roger Townshend, Earl Rivers and the Duke of Gloucester', *The Ricardian*, vol. VIII (1989); R. H. Helmholz, 'The Sons of Edward IV', A Cannonical Assessment of the Claim that they were Illegitimate', in *Richard III: Loyalty, Lordship and Law*, ed. P. W. Hammond (London, 1986); Colin Richmond, 'The Death of Edward V', *Northern History*, vol. XXV (1989); and M. A. Hicks, 'Did Edward V Outlive His Reign or Did He Outreign His Life?', *The Ricardian*, vol. IX (1990); are to be recommended.

Alison Hanham, *Richard III and his early historians 1483–1535* (Oxford, 1975), is an excellent introduction to the narrative source material. *The Crowland Chronicle Continuations 1495–1486*, ed. Nicholas Pronay and John Cox (London, 1986); Dominic Mancini, *The Usurpation of Richard III*, ed. C. A. J. Armstrong (Oxford, 1969); Thomas More, *The History of King Richard III*, ed. R. S. Sylvester, Yale Edition of the Complete Works, vol. II (1963) are good for contemporary accounts.

Two important documentary sources for the usurpation have been published with invaluable introductions: *British Library Harleian Manuscript 433*, ed. Rosemary Horrox and P. W. Hammond, four volumes (London, 1979); 'Financial Memoranda of the Reign of Edward V. Longleat Miscellaneous Manuscript Book II', ed. Rosemary Horrox, in *Camden Miscellany*, vol. XXIX (1987).

Also of great value is *The Coronation of Richard III: the Extant Documents*, ed. Anne Sutton and P. W. Hammond (Gloucester, 1983). This contains a full and annotated chronology of events 9 April–8 July 1483.

Chapter IV

THE GOVERNMENT OF RICHARD III

Rosemary Horrox

I N THE MIDDLE AGES kings ruled. It is therefore a commonplace
that one can discuss the government of Richard III, or of any
other king, as though it was distinctively 'his': shaped by the
stamp of a unique personality. In reality this is only partly true.
Medieval kings of England had the support of a central bureaucracy
which had developed its own procedures and could, in routine matters
at least, function adequately without direct intervention from the
king. Indeed, it had to: no king could literally govern his country
single-handed. Much government business thus continued virtually
unchanged from reign to reign. More important, government is always the art of the possible, and what was possible changed relatively
slowly in the Middle Ages. One should not, therefore, expect to find
dramatic changes in the underlying nature of government between
reigns. But, when all that is admitted, government *was* the king's.
The officials were his, and he could override their normal routines if
he chose. In any case, bureaucracy was only one dimension of royal
government. Much of what the king did was achieved in less formal
ways, entailing what would now be called man management, and here
the king's personality and ability were crucial; giving a very distinct
'feel', not only to different reigns, but sometimes to different periods
within the same reign.

Richard III had officials to record and transmit his wishes, authenticated by the appropriate royal seal; they also collected his revenues,

made payments, and balanced the accounts. But the sophistica-
tion with which the king's business was recorded contrasts with an
apparent lack of muscle when it came to carrying it out. Medieval
kings had no police force, no standing army — in short no professional
enforcement agencies. If a king wished to seize the land of a rebel, he
had the machinery for writing an order to that effect and making
copies of the order for his central records. He had messengers who
would carry the order to its destination, and receivers and auditors to
account for the revenues once the land had been taken into his hands.
But who was to carry out the actual seizure?

The answer, in theory, is simple. Medieval kings relied on other
people to act for them at a local level. This usually meant men of
independent influence, who were expected to use their own standing
and their own contacts to ensure that the order was carried out. The
nobility were the obvious source of such support in major matters, but
for the minutiae of local government the king looked instead to lesser
figures: to the gentry, leading townsmen and lawyers — anyone, in
fact, who happened to have influence and who was in the right place
the right time. When, in December 1483, Richard III decided that
some of the land of the executed Earl Rivers should be restored to the
abbey of St James at Northampton, the order was sent to the Sheriff of
Northamptonshire, the king's official representative in the county,
but the seizure itself was accomplished with the 'counsel and assistance' of eleven other leading men of the region, including two who
had probably been servants of Rivers himself.

Although anyone with useful influence might find themselves
appealed to in this way, medieval kings also had acknowledged
servants, who were employed on a more regular basis. The Yorkist
kings tended to formalize their relationship with such men by giving
them office within their household. This meant that they were
expected to spend some of their time at court, waiting upon the king,
but for the rest of the year they would be at home, where they were
available to act for the king as required. Numerically, there were never
enough of them to meet all the king's needs in local matters, even if this

8 William Catesby, Richard III's right-hand man.

9 *The court of the King's Bench in session at Westminster Hall.*

10 *One of the Eton College Chapel wall paintings showing a court scene in the dress of the time of the Yorkist kings.*

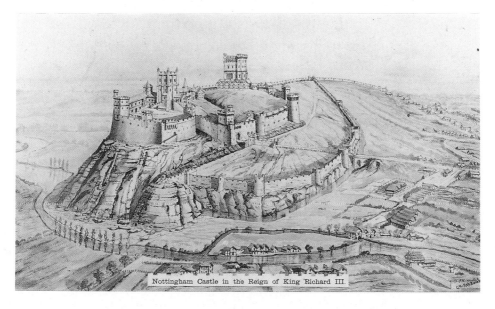

Nottingham Castle in the Reign of King Richard III.

11 *A fifteenth-century drawing of Nottingham Castle. Despite Richard III's building plans, little remains that is firmly identifiable as his.*

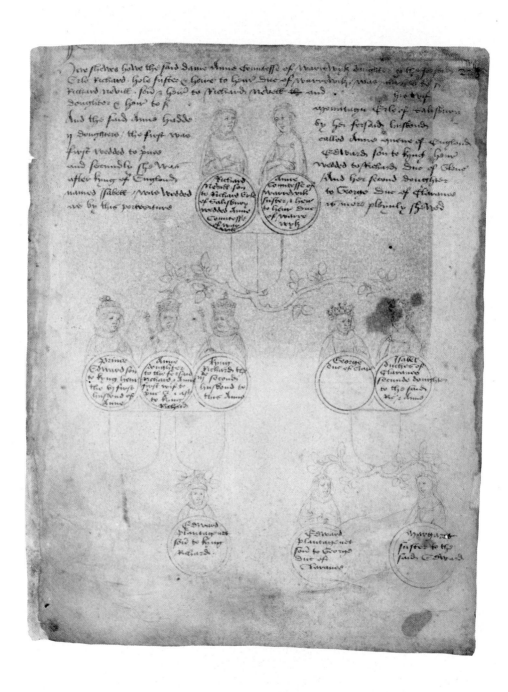

12 *The* Beauchamp Pageant: *a page celebrating the descent of Richard III's queen and son from the earls of Warwick.*

had been thought desirable, but they usually took on the most sensitive assignments. Richard III's esquire of the body, Robert Brackenbury, was not only Lieutenant of the Tower of London, itself a major responsibility, but also performed a multitude of *ad hoc* tasks, which ranged from helping to administer an oath of loyalty in Kent, to escorting Richard's bastard son to Calais. Indeed, Brackenbury was kept so busy by his royal master that in 1484 he had to delegate the job of seizing land in Kent because he was occupied with 'other arduous business touching the king's right'. Local household men also offered a way of keeping an eye on the efforts of men less closely identified with the king. Of the eleven Northamptonshire men who seized Rivers' land for St James' Abbey, three were members of Richard's household, including one of his closest allies, William Catesby.

When the king ordered men to act on his behalf, he was in some sense delegating his own authority. His command could legitimate actions — like seizing land — which would be unacceptable if performed by a subject for his own benefit. Men acting for the king also had a claim on other people's support, so that they were able to achieve more than by their unaided efforts. The household men in particular, because of their close personal identification with the king, could often find themselves carrying major responsibilities which their 'private' status would not justify. But, even so, it remains true that in a very literal sense the king's power was other people's power.

Inevitably, this meant that kings sometimes had trouble in getting things done. All kings, even the most successful, suffered from men ignoring commands or dragging their feet over carrying them out. Richard III was unable to bring the bailiffs of Pevensey to book for extortions allegedly practised on his tenants in the lordship. A letter ordering them to appear before the appropriate royal council was 'disobeyed with unfitting words and demeaning, to our great displeasure'. When two of the offenders were discovered to be actually visiting the palace of Westminster, they were again commanded in the king's name to appear before the council, 'the which they, nothing dreading, obstinately disobeyed'. In the end, Richard had to order the

Earl of Arundel, Constable of the Cinque Ports, to arrest them as a way of ensuring their appearance to answer the charges.

In general, however, kings were obeyed by most of the people most of the time. Obedience was partly dictated by self-interest. The king was the ultimate source of favour in a competitive world and carrying out his wishes earned his good will, and possibly a tangible reward (money, office or even land) as well. In any case, most men liked to be seen to be acting on the king's behalf. It demonstrated that they were people who counted in local affairs, and thereby enhanced their standing in the eyes of their neighbours. But, alongside these selfish considerations, there was also a strong sense that the king *should* be obeyed. He stood for law and stability and to ignore his commands was to threaten social order itself.

Given these pressures towards obedience, even unpopular or mis-guided royal commands might well be carried out. As a result, medieval kings display surprising political resilience, in spite of their lack of coercive power. But no king could afford to take obedience entirely for granted. It might be extremely rare for subjects to withdraw their obedience to the point where royal authority ceased to be viable, but it could happen, as Edward II had found in 1326. There was thus a corresponding pressure on kings to rule in a way which was broadly acceptable to the men upon whom they relied for action. This did not just mean winning the support of individuals by marks of favour, although patronage of this type had its place in royal government. It was, more importantly, a matter of the king identify-ing himself with his leading subjects, so that they could feel confident that his power would be used in their best interests.

This dependence on the practical backing of his subjects meant that no medieval king could be absolute in any meaningful sense of the word. But it also meant more than this. If the king's power is other people's power, then those other people must themselves be power-ful. The traditional assumption that the effectiveness of a medieval king is to be measured by the extent to which he took power away from other people and kept it for himself is thus the reverse of the truth. If the concept of a 'strong' king means anything at all, it is not a king with a monopoly of power, but rather one who was able to exploit power possessed independently of him. Indeed, successful kings generally enhanced, rather than eroded, the power of their leading subjects. On the other hand, the creation of new men, who owed their power entirely to the king, was not necessarily the attractive policy which historians often assume. It is true that such men are likely to be particularly responsive to the royal wishes, but that was not very helpful if they lacked the power and contacts which the king needed to exploit.

When he took the throne in 1483 Richard III was following a king, his brother Edward IV, who had been a master of the sort of relationships outlined above. Although with hindsight it is impossible to forget that the Yorkist dynasty outlived Edward by only a little over two years, this should not be allowed to diminish his achievements. He re-established political stability after the chaos of the closing years of Henry VI's reign, and he did so largely by creating a network of loyal servants throughout England. Among them were nobles, men like Gloucester himself, or Edward's friend and chamberlain, William Lord Hastings, who were encouraged to dominate a whole region on the king's behalf. The high political profile of such men means that they also dominate discussion of the reign, but they made up only a tiny proportion of Edward's allies. They were underpinned by a much larger group of acknowledged royal servants drawn from the gentry and below. Edward was famous for his knowledge of the men who mattered at a local level; 'even if', said a contemporary, 'they were only of yeoman status'. He took several hundred men into his household, so forging a vital link between the court and the provinces.

The existence of this network of royal servants was an important factor in Richard's decision to take the throne in 1483. At one level, it was the expression of Edward's reassertion of royal authority, and Richard may well have felt that he was the man best fitted to maintain that authority. On a more practical level, almost all of them had supported him as protector, and he probably believed that they would

THE KING'S HOUSEHOLD

THE HOUSEHOLD was formally divided into the *domus magnificencie* and the *domus providencie,* effectively the household above and below stairs, the former honourable and the latter more menial, though the senior posts in the *domus providencie* were also held by men of standing. Excluding those whose service was entirely domestic and menial there were probably at least 600 people attached to Richard's household.

In peacetime, expenditure on the household was the single biggest item of royal expenditure. The *Black Book* of Edward IV's household was compiled *c.* 1471–2 largely in order to reassert control over costs. Even so, it occasionally — as in the following extracts — alludes to the vital political role of the household men, notably as contacts between the court and the 'countries', i.e. the localities:

> Squires of the household, forty — or more if the king pleases — to be chosen with the advice of his council from men of possession, worship and wisdom; also to be of sundry shires by whom the disposition of the countries may be known. Twenty of these to be at court attending upon the king's person, in riding and going at all times and to help serve his table...
>
> It hath ever been customary for the squires to be required to wear the king's livery for the more glory and worship of this honourable household...
>
> The squires of the household of old be accustomed, winter and summer, in afternoons and in evenings, to draw to lords' chamber within court, there to keep honest company according to their skills, in talking of

go on supporting him as king, giving him a ready-made power base throughout England.

That was to prove the major misjudgement of Richard's career. Although his assumption of power met with little overt opposition in the short term, it soon became apparent that many men had acquiesced only for as long as it took to concert resistance. In October 1483 there was a major rebellion in the southern counties, aimed initially at restoring Edward V and then — when it came to be believed that Edward and his brother were dead — at establishing Henry Tudor as king.

chronicles of kings and other policies, or in piping or harping, singing, or other laudable acts, to help occupy the court and entertain guests till the time require of departing...

Knights of the Household, twelve — or more if the king pleases — the most valiant men of that order of every country...

Knowing the 'disposition of the countries' and closely attached to the person of the king, the key members of his household were uniquely well placed to wield influence, even to tell a king to his face what he did not want to hear, as the following episode, related by the Crowland Chronicler, reveals:

Eventually the king's plan and his intention to marry Elizabeth, his close kinswoman, was related to some who were opposed to it and, after the council had been summoned, the king was compelled to make his excuses at length, saying that such a thing had never entered his mind. There were those at that council who knew well enough that the contrary was true. Those who were most strongly against this marriage and whose wills the king scarcely ever dared oppose were Sir Richard Ratcliffe (a knight of the body) and William Catesby, squire of the body. These men told the king to his face that if he did not issue a public denial ... the northerners, in whom he placed greatest trust, would all rise against him ... Shortly before Easter [1485] therefore the king in the presence of the mayor and citizens of London, in a clear loud voice carried out in full the advice to make such a denial, and — as many people believed — more by the will of these counsellors than of his own volition.

The rebellion was the decisive event of Richard's reign, shattering his assumed security and dictating his actions for the rest of the reign. In the event, it collapsed without ever seriously threatening Richard's grasp of his new kingdom, but its implications were far more damaging than this might suggest. The risings did not only involve men like the Woodvilles, whom Richard had pushed from power and whose disaffection was predictable. It also drew in many of the leading men of Edward IV's household: men whom Richard had kept in post and upon whom he had been relying to act as a focus for his own authority in the south of England. Some of these men had personal motives for rebellion. Thomas Arundel of Lanherne (Cornwall), for instance, was involved in a land dispute with Richard's associate James Tyrell and may well have feared that any decision would now be in his rival's favour. But rebellion against a crowned king was always a huge step, and the readiness of men to take it in 1483 suggests real doubts about the validity of Richard's regime, even where distaste for his seizure of power was not itself a primary motive.

Within a matter of months of his taking the throne, therefore, Richard was faced with reconstructing his power in the southern half of his realm. His response was to turn to men he knew he could trust, men who had been associated with him as Duke of Gloucester and who were in many cases from the north of England. To give them influence in the South, Richard used the land and office forfeited by the 1483 rebels to construct power bases for them. John Hoton of county Durham stepped into William Berkeley's shoes in Hampshire. Edward Redmane of Harewood (Yorkshire), based himself at Cotehele, the former home of the rebel Richard Edgecombe. Some thirty men received endowments of this sort, and they in turn brought others south with them, who might receive lesser grants to settle them in their new areas.

The use of such men to reassert royal influence in the South was bitterly resented. The issue was not simply that they were 'outsiders'. Medieval society was far from parochial and movement from region to region was not uncommon. The rebel Roger Tocotes of Bromham (Wiltshire), for instance, was himself a northerner, who had moved south by marriage. But Richard's allies were being forced into local society through the exclusion of established families. The arrival of the newcomers, and particularly the use of forfeited land to endow them, amounted to a considerable social upheaval. Land was status and its safe descent from generation to generation was the central concern of the men who constituted the king's chief allies: the nobility, gentry and professional classes. Interference in its smooth descent produced a sort of tenurial queasiness, reminding other landowners that they too might be vulnerable.

In Richard's case, this uneasiness may have been compounded by the element of deliberate political engineering on the king's part. Richard was not just rewarding his friends at the expense of his enemies. He was artificially creating local influence which he could then exploit. This generated resentment in itself. It was strongly felt that local government, at whatever level, should be in the hands of men with a stake in the area. Richard's plantation of men in the South testifies to his acceptance of this view, since he was trying to establish a new generation of *local* servants. But, in the short term, until the newcomers could put down roots, Richard's reliance on them looked like an attempt to dictate events from the centre, rather than an act of co-operation between king and local subjects.

Ideologically, the plantations undoubtedly damaged the king. When he had taken power, Richard had presented himself as the man best able to preserve the good government of his brother against the threat of factionalization represented by the Woodvilles. Now, at least in the South, he had himself become associated with an alien clique and many of his brother's leading household men were excluded from power. The result was a further weakening of Richard's reputation in just the area where it most needed to be strengthened.

This helps to explain the later outbreaks of opposition to Richard in the Home Counties and the South, and as such was politically extremely harmful. The damage to the king's government, by contrast, was more limited. The rebellion had lost Richard the circle of leading household men who would normally have spearheaded royal activity in the South, which inevitably limited his ability to repair the damage done to his authority there. But local men uninvolved in the rebellion could still be found to act for the king in the normal processes of local government, such as staffing commissions or holding inquiries. This does not necessarily say anything about their attitude to Richard. In obeying the king's orders, these local gentry were, in effect, governing their own region: it was an exercise in self-government as well as royal

RICHARD III'S ITINERARY

RICHARD SPENT the two winters of his reign in London and Westminster. From spring to November he was generally to be found away from the capital, but compared with other fifteenth-century kings he spent a remarkable amount of time along the line of the Great North Road, at York, Pontefract and especially Nottingham, where he sometimes remained for months at a time. As the map shows, even after October 1483, Richard rarely showed his face in the seat of rebellion, the southern counties.

SCARBOROUGH
More than 10 days

YORK
More than 40 days

PONTEFRACT
More than 40 days

NOTTINGHAM
More than 6 months

LEICESTER
More than 10 days

KENILWORTH
More than 10 days

WINDSOR
More than 20 days

LONDON AND WESTMINSTER
More than 10 months

Counties involved in the rebellion of October 1483. (Berkshire, Brecon, Cornwall, Devon, Dorset, Essex, Hampshire, Kent, Oxford, Somerset, Surrey, Sussex, Wiltshire.)

government. The justices of the peace, for instance, were appointed at the centre and their selection signalled royal trust of the men chosen, but in upholding law and order they were performing what they regarded as their proper role as the leaders of local society.

There were also men in the counties affected by the rebellion who were prepared to take a more active part in royal service. Although the incomers tend to dominate the politically sensitive assignments, Richard was never entirely dependent on them. In Gloucestershire, for instance, Richard took Giles Brigge of Coberley into his household and used him to investigate treason in the county. Exactly why such men backed Richard cannot usually be determined. Some probably had personal links with the new king or his circle. Piers St Aubyn, in Cornwall, may have been an associate of James Tyrell, for instance. However, in many cases it is likely that Richard was simply benefiting from the principle that the king should be obeyed. Obedience to the king was not only a matter of personal friendship and loyalty — although that produced the most reliable service — it also had an institutional dimension.

This can be seen within the royal household itself, where a number of the men whom Richard inherited from his brother remained obedient allies without, it seems, ever being particularly close to the king. But it is, as one would expect, most marked within the central administration. Here, continuity between reigns had become the norm by this date. In part, this is no doubt because kings were unwilling to lose the expertise built up in a previous reign, but it probably also owes something to a growing professionalism among the bureaucrats themselves, which meant that they saw themselves as servants of the king — whoever he happened to be — rather than of an individual.

There were exceptions to this pattern. The great officers of state, men like the chancellor or the treasurer of the exchequer, were not professional administrators and, as 'political' appointments, were more vulnerable. Edward's chancellor, Archbishop Rotherham of York, was dismissed by Richard, and Richard's chancellor, John

Russell, Bishop of Lincoln, in turn lost office under Henry VII. There was also a handful of offices regarded as so closely identified with the king that their holders were unlikely to weather a change of regime. The king's secretary is the obvious example. Edward's secretary, Oliver King, had been arrested by Gloucester in June 1483. Richard's secretary, John Kendal, was attainted by Henry VII after Bosworth and, although he probably survived the battle, he disappears into obscurity. But, on the whole, the staff of the central offices worked steadily up the promotion ladder, serving whoever happened to be giving the orders at the time.

As all this suggests, although Richard's title to the throne was disputed and some of his actions criticized, his regime never ceased to be viable. Behind the high-profile defections, the great majority of people in both central and local government circles remained willing to act on his behalf. Richard's tendency to rely on a small circle of supporters for politically sensitive tasks left some of his allies over-extended, but there never came a point when his wishes could not be met. In the twenty-six months that Richard was King of England, government continued much as normal. What did the king achieve in that time?

To modern eyes, the range of government activity in the Middle Ages seems limited. The best contemporary definition is that of Sir John Fortescue who, having experienced the system from the inside, summed up the king's role as to preserve the peace outward and inward. In other words, the king was responsible for the defence of the realm and, more broadly, for foreign policy. He was also charged with the preservation of law and order at home, which was not confined to upholding the formal process of law, but involved maintaining political and, in theory, social stability.

Richard III's public statements show that he shared this perception of the king's role. He wanted to be seen as the leader who would unite his people against a shared enemy: 'that prince ... [who] is disposed to employ his own royal person as far as ever any king hath done in years past, to the encouraging of his faithful subjects and confusion of all his enemies'. It must have been a major disappointment that he never had the opportunity to wage a foreign war. When he came to the throne, England was at war with Scotland and there was an incipient state of war against France. But, for financial and political reasons, Richard had to disengage from both and instead found himself in arms against his own subjects.

Richard also identified himself strongly with the maintenance of the law — and with the 'rest and peace and quiet' of his subjects to which the rule of law could be expected to lead. In so doing, he was making a general statement of intent, rather than laying down a programme for legal reform, although his reign did see an important tidying up of some aspects of land law. As king, the law was his and he sat in judgement in King's Bench at least once, but, for the most part, support for the law meant leaving the judiciary to get on with it. A king's impact was generally more direct in the wider field of order: a concept which embraced the king's own security as well as that of his subjects, since it was taken for granted that the king's stability was a prerequisite of order. Here, Richard's commitment was clearly sincere, but his success limited. The rebellions, followed as they were by confiscations and less formal score-settling, meant that in the short term Richard seemed to have worsened the situation rather than to have improved it.

The other main area in which Richard was active was finance: a subject close to any king's heart. It had also been a central concern of Edward IV, whose policies Richard largely followed. The main administrative development of Edward's reign had been the emergence of the chamber — the king's private apartments — as a financial agency alongside the exchequer. Revenue from various sources, notably the Crown estates, was paid directly into the chamber — in effect to the king himself — and was available there for him to spend as he chose. The system was dependent on the king's own interest and it collapsed at Edward's death, but Richard recognized its value and promptly revived it.

It was not only the handling of finance which Edward IV reformed. He also made efforts to increase the Crown's income from its own resources and it is a measure of his success that he was able to do without parliamentary taxation for much of the later part of his reign. His reserves were, however, drained by war against Scotland and in the last months of his reign he was forced not only to ask Parliament for taxation, but also to resort to benevolences (forced gifts to the Crown). This renewed financial pressure was extremely unpopular and explains why Richard, in spite of inheriting an empty treasury from his brother, outlawed benevolences and refrained from asking Parliament for a grant of taxation.

The gesture was a good public relations move, but it left Richard in financial difficulties for the rest of his reign. Like his brother, he tried to step up the yield from the Crown lands. Rents were reconsidered and new tenants often found themselves paying more than their predecessors. Guidelines were drawn up for increasing the profitability of land in the king's hands and making sure that the benefit came to the king, rather than into the pockets of his local officials. Royal park officials in the honour of Tutbury, for instance, lost the perk of unlimited grazing for their own animals and could now keep only two horses and two cows. Richard also tried to exploit his feudal rights more efficiently. Edward IV had already made a beginning, but Richard apparently intended to put the attempt on a more formal basis. In March 1485, he appointed commissioners to investigate concealed royal rights in the south-west; a forerunner of more elaborate Tudor innovations in the same field.

In the long term, as the Tudors were to demonstrate, such methods could produce a rich yield for the Crown. In the short term, it was not enough to rescue Richard from his financial problems. In spring 1485, Richard had to resort to raising a national loan. He was within his rights in doing so — the benevolences he had outlawed in Parliament were gifts, not loans, to the Crown — but the move was bound to be unpopular and the fact that Richard made the attempt is evidence of real financial trouble. The loan was intended to raise around £30,000, probably rather more than the annual disposable income from the Crown lands. What is actually raised is unknown. About £2,000 can be traced in the records of the exchequer, but most was probably paid straight into the chamber, for which no records survive.

The financial tactics of the Yorkist kings demanded detailed knowledge of their land and their subjects, and the importance of acquiring that information is the subtext of Richard's recommendations for financial reform. Knowledge was also power when it came to deciding which local men to use in royal business. A king who was out of touch — or, of course, deliberately misinformed — would not be fully effective. By the fifteenth century, when kings were far less peripatetic than they had been in previous centuries, their main channel for obtaining this information was the royal household. Edward IV's household ordinances admit as much, recommending that servants be drawn from a wide geographical range, 'by whom the disposition of the countries may be known'. The court must have hummed with the exchange of news, although by its very nature gossip leaves relatively little trace in formal records.

It was not only information which needed to reach the king; his subjects also had to be able to approach him. The king was the ultimate source of help in a dangerous and competitive world. If one had to sum up the king's role in a single phrase, it would be that he was the man who settled problems which no one else could handle. The king's time was far more likely to be spent listening to a stream of requests and complaints than sitting in a back room making policy. Richard himself attached considerable value to this accessibility. When he visited Kent after the 1483 rebellion, he announced that 'every person ... that finds himself grieved, oppressed or unlawfully wronged do make a bill of his complaint, and put it to his highness, and he shall be heard.'

The king's decision-making was not done single-handed. He was expected to take advice. Much consultation was no doubt relatively casual, with the king sounding the opinion of men around him. He also had a formal council to advise him on major issues. Its own records do not survive for this period, but it can occasionally be glimpsed in action, agreeing to the appointment of ambassadors, or taking sureties of good conduct from former rebels. Richard, following his brother's

Raising Money

I N FEBRUARY 1485, Richard, still determined not to tax his subjects, decided to raise money by borrowing from them. Commissioners were appointed and were provided with letters with which they were to approach potential lenders:

> Sir, the king's grace greeteth you well and desireth and heartily prayeth you that by way of loan ye will let him have such sum as his grace hath written to you. And ye shall truly have again at such days as he hath showed and promised to you in his letters, and this he desireth to be employed for the defence and security of his Royal person and for the well-being of this his Realm. And for that intent his grace and all his lords thinking that every true Englishman will help him in this behalf, of which number his grace reputeth and taketh you for one. And that is the cause he thus writeth to you before other for the great love, confidence and substance that his grace hath and knoweth in you, which trusteth undoubtedly that ye like a loving subject will at this time accomplish this his desire.

How many of the king's true subjects responded as Richard hoped, and how much was raised in this way, is not known. Perhaps they were

precedent, also established regional councils: one in the North headed by his nephew John de la Pole; another, almost certainly, at Calais, nominally headed by his illegitimate son John.

All the councils could take decisions on the king's behalf, but in the end it was always the king's decision which counted, and the question of who influenced him was accordingly crucial. It was an inevitable consequence of personal monarchy that the king would rather listen to some people than others and, on the whole, men seeking royal help or favour accepted that and made their arrangements accordingly. Under Edward IV everyone knew that Hastings was the man who could 'do with the king', and that fact made Hastings' fortune. But if it was felt that access to the king was being blocked, or that the influence of his friends was too blatantly one-sided, then criticism would soon grow. There may have been some uneasiness on this score in flattered by being told of the king's great love for them, but it is note-worthy that Richard does not appear to have tried his brother's much more personal approach. This, for instance, is how an Italian merchant, Battesta Oldovini de Brugnato, writing from London in 1475 to a friend of his in Milan, described Edward IV's methods when he was aiming to persuade people, not to lend him money, but to give it:

> I have many times seen our neighbours here who were called before the king; when they went they looked as though they were going to the gallows; when they returned they were elated, saying that they had talked with the king; and because he had spoken to them so many kind words, they did not regret the money they had paid.

Because, Battesta concluded, Edward gave each visitor 'a very great welcome as though he had always known him ... everyone seemed to pay willingly ... He has plucked the feathers from the magpies without making them cry out.'

Undoubtedly, like all effective devices for raising money, Edward's could be — and probably was — over-used; but that there is no record of Richard attempting a similar personal touch says much for their very different styles of man management.

Richard's reign. William Collingbourne's famous couplet points the finger at the inner circle at court: 'The Cat, the Rat and Lovell our Dog/ Rule all England under the Hog.' The influence of the men he names, William Catesby, Richard Ratcliffe and Francis Lovell, is confirmed by the Crowland Chronicler, the best informed of the early writers on Richard's reign.

Assessing Richard's government is not easy. His reign is simply too short and the pressures posed by opposition to the king means that there is inevitably a gap between Richard's expressed aims and his achievements. He was not the great reforming king that some of his defenders have claimed, but then under the circumstances it would be unreasonable to expect him to be. It is also worth pointing out that that does not seem to be how Richard wanted to be seen. Medieval society, with its emphasis (however factitious) on the value of precedent and tradition, was not disposed to welcome radical new brooms. 'Good' government worked within accepted parameters and it is no accident that Richard, who was well aware of society's expectations, began his reign by emphasizing that he stood for continuity.

That commitment to continuity was partly ideological, since it was Richard's justification for seizing power in the first place. But it was also the practical reality. Everything Richard did grew out of his brother's strategy. Even his plantation of men in the South, which for some contemporaries seemed such a radical departure, was the logical consequence of Richard's adoption of Edward's goal of a strong household presence in each county. Richard III surely saw himself as the torch-bearer for Yorkist government, and it is on those terms that he needs to be judged. In the event, of course, he destroyed the House of York and that dynastic disaster inevitably overshadows his reign. Had he won at Bosworth, he would probably have succeeded in building on his brother's achievements. As it was, Henry Tudor was to do that.

FURTHER READING

Rosemary Horrox, *Richard III: A Study of Service* (Cambridge, 1989); David Morgan, 'The house of policy: the political role of the late Plantagenet household' in *The English Court from the Wars of the Roses to the Civil War*, ed. David Starkey (London, 1987) and 'The King's Affinity in the Polity of Yorkist England', *Transactions of the Royal Historical Society* 5th series 23 (1973); A. R. Myers, *The Household of Edward IV* (Manchester, 1959); Tony Pollard, 'The Tyranny of Richard III', *Journal of Medieval History* 3 (1977); C. D. Ross, *Richard III* (London, 1981) — especially chapters 9–10; Anne Sutton, '"A Curious Searcher for our Weal Public": Richard III, Piety, Chivalry and the Concept of the "Good Prince"' in *Richard III, Loyalty, Lordship and the Law*, ed. P. W. Hammond (London, 1986); B. P. Wolffe, *The Royal Demesne in English History* (London, 1971) and *The Crown Lands, 1485–1536* (London, 1970).

Chapter v

THE COURT AND ITS CULTURE
IN THE REIGN OF RICHARD III

Anne F. Sutton

... to show unto you ... our intent and pleasure for to have you to use the manner of our English habit and clothing, for the which cause we send you ... a collar of gold of our livery and device with other apparel for your person of the English fashion ... we shall have you to come over unto us hither and be more expert both in the manner and conditions of us and other honourable and goodly behaving of our subjects.

RICHARD III'S LETTER to the Irish Earl of Desmond in 1484 shows confidence in the manners, dress and culture of his court: Desmond would benefit from contact with it. The king's instructions to Thomas Barrow, the Bishop of Annaghdown, who was to take the letter and clothes to Desmond, expanded on the political persuasions which were to be used to draw the Irishman back to English influence, but it is clear that Richard had, above all, a practical sense of what civilization was about. Desmond was to be assured that the king would send 'gowns, doublets, hosen and bonnets, and so followingly in time coming, as the case or change of the said fashion shall require ...' Nor did the king spare cost: the clothes parcel included long gowns of cloth of gold and velvet lined with satin and damask, doublets, shirts, kerchiefs, hose, bonnets and hats, and the gold collar was to cost between £20 and £30.

Richard thought of his court as civilized. He knew too that appearance was important, that fashion was ephemeral and that a courtier had to keep up with it. 'Goodly behaving', orderly personal display and ceremony were fundamental aspects of courtly culture in the fifteenth century as in any other.

This affected the king himself as well as his great lords, like Desmond, for it was by the means of ceremony, etiquette and organized display that the culture, dignity and power of the king was exhibited within his own country and to foreign princes abroad. He was advertising the status and strength of himself and his kingdom. His subjects expected him to spend his wealth in this way:

> Item, it shall need that the king have such treasure, as he may make new buildings when he will, for his pleasure and magnificence; and as he may buy him rich clothes, rich furs ... rich stones ... and other jewels and ornaments convenient to his estate royal. And often times he will buy rich hangings and other apparel for his houses; ... vessel, vestments ... for his chapel; buy also horses of great price, trappers, and do other such noble and great costs as besuiteth his royal majesty ... For if a king did not so ... he liveth not like his estate ... [Sir John Fortescue]

The 'Lantern of England'

THE COURT or household of the king was the 'lantern of England'. It not only lit England itself, but also made England famous and 'visible' abroad. The phrase was used by the *Black Book* which described the elaborate structure of officials surrounding Edward IV. It was divided into a household above stairs, *domus magnificencie*, and one below stairs, the domestic or provisioning side, the *domus providencie*. It provided the king and his family — although a queen had her own, smaller household — with the necessities and luxuries of daily life and its officers carried out his wishes and enabled him to rule the country. Officers of the court included nobles, knights and esquires, whose sons might be among the privileged 'henchmen' in attendance on the king and educated in the court, and whose daughters might serve the queen. To function properly, this large organization needed to be kept under control, the lord chamberlain and the steward presiding above and below stairs respectively. The lord chamberlain was particularly close to the king, because of his duties, and was often a personal friend: Francis, Lord Lovell, held this office under Richard III.

Ceremony and etiquette were also a means of maintaining discipline. In such matters, the court which was most admired and imitated in the fifteenth century was that of the Valois dukes of Burgundy, also lords of the Low Countries. Richard III had visited it twice and his sister, Margaret, had married the last duke, Charles, killed in 1477. Before Richard became king, however, the character of this great court had changed for ever and it had lost its pre-eminent role in culture and politics. Olivier de la Marche, master of ceremonies to the last two dukes (and a master of business organization and personnel management), found his world altered and wished that he had not lived to see the change. He could no longer take comfort in his carefully arranged courtly displays which had reflected so well the peace and unity achieved under the authority of such powerful rulers as the last dukes, now largely destroyed by civil and foreign war and a minority. In contrast, the safe island of England, despite damaging spurts of civil war, never lacked a king, and the king's court was as effective at displaying royal authority under the Yorkists as under Henry VII.

Ceremony and Display

THERE WERE great moments of ceremony and display throughout Richard's reign. There is no sign that Richard, his queen or his court rejected any of the panoply and richness of royal rank.

After the coronation, Richard took his court on a tour through the country; he needed to show the people that it was he who was king, and not the expected Edward V, and that his rule would be beneficial. A series of royal entries introduced him to the leading cities, just as the coronation procession from the Tower to Westminster had shown him to the capital. The royal entry was one of the most useful means available to a monarch for the display of his power and authority, and the Yorkist kings used it with as much effect as such image-conscious

THE CORONATION OF RICHARD III

THE CORONATION set the scene for the reign. It was a ceremony founded on traditions and, like his predecessors, Richard paid attention to them all: he dined in state in the Tower, he created knights of the Bath, and he and his queen rode in procession to Westminster. The magnificence of the occasion was amplified by the mere fact that he had a queen to be crowned and many of the ceremonies had to be duplicated. All the essential liturgy was enacted, the king was anointed, took his oath, was crowned and afterwards feasted. Richard made what appear to be two innovations to the ceremonies: he took the oath in English for the first time; and he decided that the holy oil, given by the Virgin Mary to St Thomas Becket, should in future be housed with the other regalia in Westminster Abbey. These two personal interventions in the coronation ceremonial are the first of the few indications of Richard's own cultural interests and choices: he was capable of rejecting the traditional French of the oath in the interests of clarity and understanding, and he revered relics and religious ceremonial.

rulers as Henry V, Elizabeth I or Philip and Charles of Burgundy in their own day. The king could thereby extend his splendour and the civilization of his court — the 'lantern of England' — to a wider circle of his subjects than usual. It was such a successful precedent, that Henry VII imitated it in 1485. On his tour, Richard showed particular marks of favour to certain towns: at Oxford he attended learned disputations; Gloucester was given a charter; and York was honoured as the place where he chose to create his son Prince of Wales. York's leading citizens and clergy were drawn into the ceremony and 13,000 white boars cut out of cloth, the king's personal badge, were distributed to spectators. The city responded by staging a magnificent reception for him and later put on a special performance of its Creed play. The rebellions of the autumn cut short the king's progress, but in January he was able to resume this convivial and splendid role. He invited the citizens of London to his Epiphany feast when he wore his crown in the White Hall. He not only presented the mayor with a gold cup set with pearls and gems, but also offered to make the borough of Southwark part of the city's jurisdiction. Richard was rewarding the citizens for their financial assistance, and he was also, like Edward IV before him, adeptly making available the luxuries of his court — its wines, cooking, fine napery, music and good manners — beyond its usual aristocratic confines, and welcoming to it his merchants and townsmen.

One important court ceremony over which Richard appears never to have presided was the St George's day feast of the Order of the Garter at Windsor. In 1484, the feast day, 23 April, was a couple of weeks after the death of the Prince of Wales and not until 24 April did Richard order, belatedly, that the usual livery be issued. In 1485, on the day before the feast, Richard sent word to Lord Maltravers that he was to observe the ceremonial in full in the king's absence. Perhaps this time it was the period of mourning for the queen, who had died about six weeks before, that prevented his presence. No personal disinclination for this feast or the ceremonies of chivalry is likely: Richard had held the supreme chivalric post of constable as Duke of Gloucester and had shown great interest in the work of the royal heralds, the experts in chivalry. He had overseen the drawing up of ordinances which encouraged the heralds to cultivate manners and eloquence and record contemporary feats of arms and ceremonies. As king, Richard gave them a charter of incorporation and the house of Coldharbour as their headquarters. Heralds acted as ambassadors and travelled the courts of Europe; they not only organized processions, tournaments and anything involving precedence, they also recorded rank and pedigree, both matters of passionate interest and pride to most of the English court. Much of the contemporary love of history centred on the glorification of one's own family: the *Beauchamp Pageant* and the *Rous Roll*, both made in Richard's reign, celebrated the Beauchamp family. The *Salisbury Roll* (compiled in the 1460s and copied in Richard's reign) was a beautifully illustrated descent of the earldom of Salisbury, also held by ancestors of his queen. Other families had their own pompous pedigrees and many nobles kept personal heralds, such as the Duke of Buckingham's 'Percival' and Richard of Gloucester's 'Blanc Sanglier'.

At Christmas 1484, the clerical author of the Crowland *Chronicle* remembered that 'far too much attention was given to dancing and gaiety and vain changes of apparel presented to Queen Anne and the Lady Elizabeth ...' Any observer, whether a disenchanted cleric or a foreign ambassador, tended to remember the conduct of court festivals, the very essence of court life, and also the monarch's clothes — the same cleric was able to detail a major change in fashion during Edward IV's time. Precise records of the clothes of the Yorkist kings are few. What was probably the main coronation garment of an English king in the 1480s can be seen in the surviving Eton Chapel wall paintings: a long, loose gown with enormous sleeves lined throughout with fur (purple velvet and thickly powdered ermine), with an imperial crown and sceptre. The only visual record of the Yorkist court are these wall-paintings and the drawings of the *Pageant* of the life of Richard Beauchamp, Earl of Warwick, commissioned probably for his great-grandson, Richard III's Prince of Wales.

A king wore the rarest and most expensive silks and furs unless his personal character was as unusual as that of Louis XI who preferred to dress like a common huntsman.

> It is right well seeming unto a king, that he be royal and excellent in his array, so that ever he show him in rich and precious clothing, and that his clothing be of the most strange cloth that may ... be found; and that is a great prerogative ... that he surmount all other lords ... in his royal array ... (*Secreta Secretorum*).

Philip the Good of Burgundy (died 1467) chose to wear black for most events and for most of his reign, either out of affectation or perhaps to remember the murder of his father. He laid it aside for special occasions such as the Feast of the Pheasant or a May Day. A pure, deep black was one of the most difficult colours for the dyer to achieve so it was automatically one of the most expensive and luxurious of colours; it was also a superb foil for gold, jewels and furs. For Richard's clothes the evidence is meagre. Only five gowns are recorded for him apart from his coronation robes. Four were of crimson cloth of gold of various patterns, all lined with green damask, satin or velvet; one of these was worn during the ceremony for the creation of thePrince of Wales. He had a magnificent gown of purple cloth of gold wrought with garters and roses, lined with white and, as the cloth was the gift of his queen and he gave her a gift of purple cloth of gold upon damask in return, they probably wore them on the same state occasion soon after the coronation.

Jewels and plate were an equally important part of display and an indication of the taste of the king and his court. One of the few signs of Richard's personal preferences is the bequest to him by Sir John Pilkington in 1478 of his great emerald set in gold, for which Richard had offered as much as 100 marks (£66. 13s. 4d.). Some court jewels in the shape of Yorkist roses were illustrated in Burgundian books and paintings of the time. The coronet of Margaret of York, decorated with the white roses of her family and the monogram 'CM' for her husband Charles and herself, still survives in Aachen Cathedral, the gift of the devout duchess.

Jewels and plate were used as currency as well as gracious gifts (and persuaders) and personal adornment. Lord Howard gave Richard a gold cup in May 1483, Richard gave a good servant, William Mauleverer, a ring with a diamond, and gave (or pawned) a balas ruby with three pendant pearls to George Cely. When he was short of cash, the royal jewels he pledged included a salt cellar, a coronal, a helmet of Edward IV, all of gold and jewelled, and twelve images of the apostles in silver gilt. When not in pawn, these items adorned royal cupboards, tables and altars: Richard arranged for his northern household to have for display a gold cup with a saphire and another of jasper decorated with gold, pearls and other stones, and he gave the city of London a jewelled, gold cup to set on its cupboard at mayoral feasts.

MUSIC AT COURT

MUSIC WAS the essential accompaniment of all court ceremony, religious and secular. Like earlier kings, such as Henry VI, Richard ordered that his realm be searched for talented additions to his household musicians: John Melyonek, a gentleman of his chapel royal skilled in the 'science' of music was to visit all the cathedrals, chapels, colleges and religious houses and take any man or child of ability into the king's service. Those chosen could look forward to a prestigious career, and a boy whose voice had broken might progress to one of the universities and receive preferment.

English musicians enjoyed a high reputation abroad, the most famous, John Dunstable, worked mainly on the continent, and Robert Morton enjoyed employment at the courts of the last two Burgundian dukes. Bohemian visitors praised the quality of Edward IV's chapel choir, and the nobility emulated it in their own foundations as Richard's statutes for his College of Middleham testify. There was a continuous exchange of

'Goodly Behaving' and Courtly Accomplishments

MUSIC MAKING was a required accomplishment of the courtier, especially those who had had the good fortune to be educated in the king's household, 'the school of urbanity and nurture of England'. The education of these favoured henchmen of the king (and the queen) was part of the daily life of the court and they were among the regular entourage of the king. Elaborate regulations for their training are recorded in the *Black Book* of Edward IV's household. The boys' subjects of study show that courtiers were expected to be of use to their monarch in diplomacy, administration and war, as well as pleasant and cultivated companions. They were to learn the harp, 'to pipe, sing, dance, and ... other honest and temperate behaving,' and 'to ride cleanly and surely,' to joust and wear armour. The essential military textbook they read was Vegetius's *De Re Militari* (On Military Matters) of which a copy was commissioned by, or given to, Richard for his son. Vegetius gave much advice on the athletic training of adolescent youths. Proper attention was also to be paid to 'courtesy in minstrels across the Channel and when there was a great festival in the offing more turned up in the hope of a job. Nichodemus, a trumpeter from Rome, secured employment at Richard's coronation. Safe-conducts issued by the king show minstrels of the Duke of Austria and from Bavaria travelling home from work in England; Robert of Beek, a royal trumpeter, probably from Guelders, travelled abroad on the king's business in December 1483. There were usually over thirteen waged minstrels in the Yorkist household; we know that John Crowland, and then Peter de Casanova, was marshal of the king's trumpeters, so important for announcing the courses of banquets and the formal entries of kings. Out of forty-seven minstrels known to have been employed at Richard III's coronation, at least thirty were trumpeters. The singers of the chapel royal not only sang at religious services, they might also perform with secular music at meals and entertainments. Some of the royal minstrels also travelled around the country, as did similar troupes patronized by leading nobles: in 1484 the town of Cambridge rewarded the minstrels of the Prince of Wales, the Duchess of York and the queen.

words, deeds and degrees,' as well as 'sundry languages and other learnings virtuous'.

If 'courtesy in words, deeds and degrees' was politeness and a knowledge of history and of the pedigree and place in society of everyone, the 'other learnings virtuous' of the courtier may have included verbal skills and the composition of verse. Those with verbal skills were prized in a period when entertainment had to be largely self-made. A little of the verse of Anthony Woodville is known and *The Assembly of Ladies* was possibly written by a lady of the Yorkist court. This poem is a charming, rather aimless allegory delighting in clothes and courtly games, one of which is to allot every character a motto.

'Sundry Languages'
ENGLAND WAS a country of three languages, Latin, French and English, and the king kept secretaries expert in each. Richard himself and his courtiers knew all three with varying degrees of skill. He used Latin, the international language of diplomacy, the Church and

---

MOTTOES

MOTTOES, or 'reasons' as they were called, were extensively used in courtly verse and entertainments and as a means of social identity. Not only did every armigerous family need a motto, but individuals had them too. The King of England began to use *dieu et mon droit* in the fifteenth century and the motto of the Order of the Garter was *honi soit qui mal y pense*. It is well known that Richard used or played with several mottoes. He and his wife may have used *a votre plaisir* (at your service, or pleasure). *A vous me lie* (it binds me to you or I bind myself to you) is in his New Testament, *tant le desirée* (I have longed for it so much) occurs in his adolescent hand in his copy of *Ipomedon,* and he used *loyaulte me lie* (loyalty binds me) in his last years as Duke of Gloucester and as king. Mottoes were used to identify oneself and one's possessions, from a single book or jewel to a whole household of servants. They were also adopted casually and temporarily in a particular game, poetry contest or tournament: at the great tournament of 1467 Anthony Woodville and Anthony, the Grand Bastard of Burgundy, displayed their mottoes on their tents.

---

scholars. Of the sixteen texts he is known to have owned, six were in Latin — among them his book of hours, from which he read his devotions, a copy remarkably free of errors in its Latin and to which he added several other Latin prayers. He listened to Latin orations from Scots ambassadors in 1484 and he attended Latin disputations at Oxford. His court was not short of learned clergy. Among them, Richard recommended John Shirwood to the Pope as Bishop of Durham, speaking of his 'integrity of life, exceptional knowledge of holy writ, outstanding knowledge of both languages, and gentle manners ...', and later tried to have him made a cardinal. Thomas Langton, 'our very dear and most faithful counsellor and spokesman who knows the secrets of our heart,' whom Richard preferred to the bishopric of Salisbury, was an enthusiastic educationalist, and John Gunthorpe, his keeper of the privy seal, had been educated in Italy and was a fine scholar.

French was the second language of diplomacy and also the language of aristocratic culture and chivalry; great romances and histories had been written in it. Edward IV spoke French so well that Philippe de Commynes remarked on it; John Howard, Richard III's Duke of Norfolk, was a practised diplomat and read French for pleasure (but he kept his household accounts in English). Richard owned two long French prose texts, a *Grandes Chroniques de France* (the standard history of France) and a *Tristan*. A degenerate or noble French dialect (depending on whether your point of view was that of a Frenchman or an English common lawyer) was still used in the English law courts and for certain legal records, the statutes of England being written in English for the first time only in Richard's reign. It is perhaps hardly surprising that the Yorkist kings failed to commission translations into English when they could read French readily and rely on the many French translations of Latin texts made for the Burgundian dukes. Edward IV bought himself over thirty of these new translations; of Richard's purchases, if any, we know nothing.

Richard's interest in English works is well attested and is probably representative of the interests of his average courtier. He owned some Chaucer and Lydgate, an English verse paraphrase of the Old Testament, a prose rendering of the twelfth-century romance of the perfect knight, *Ipomedon,* and an English translation of a German mystical work. He probably knew Langland's *Vision of Piers Plowman* well enough to quote from it and call Nottingham Castle his 'castle of care'. He received the dedication of at least one literary text, Caxton's edition of *The Order of Chivalry*.

The merchant class of England, particularly the merchant adventurers who traded abroad, had a fourth language, Dutch, the language of the Low Countries which were not only the most important possessions of the Burgundian dukes, but also vital to the English cloth and wool trade. The merchant adventurers frequented Bruges, Middelburg and the great fairs of Bergen op Zoom, Antwerp and Ghent. Anything could be bought there: tapestries from Flanders, armour and silks from Italy, illuminated books from Bruges, linens from Courtrai, Mechlin or Reims. The Merchant Adventurers maintained a permanent establishment at Bruges ruled by a governor, of which William Caxton was the most famous. In this office Caxton acted as a diplomat, as well as making a fortune as a merchant; he had connections with Edward IV and with Margaret of York. As a keen bibliophile, she took a benevolent interest in the last venture of his life, that of printing English books in England. Caxton's career shows how easily the merchant class, the English court and their European equivalents could communicate upon occasion. He knew several members of the English court and had texts recommended to him by such as Anthony Woodville. He aimed largely at the English reading market, leaving the printing of Latin or scholarly texts to the foreign entrepreneurs who were also setting up presses in England. A statute of Richard III's, which aimed to control foreigners settling in England, specifically exempted those who were printers and any who were involved in making or selling books. Few of the foreign born printers prospered for long, but Caxton's firm continued to publish books in English for sixty years. He made many of his own translations from Latin, French and Dutch: perhaps he could find no one to employ to do it better or quicker, or perhaps he just liked doing it. Certainly English texts, such as the continuation for his *Chronicles of England* up to 1461 (which he probably compiled himself), were difficult to come by. The businessman in Caxton recognized that English people with little or no French and Latin needed English books, while the aristocrat was probably still happy with a predominance of French in his or her romance and chivalric reading matter.

Foreign Influences
THE FOREIGN CONTACTS of the English court stretched further than the Low Countries. The king sent representatives to the papal court. A prosperous group of Italians lived in London comprising clergy, merchants selling the silks of Lucca, Florence and Venice, and buying English wool and cloth, and poets like Pietro Carmeliano, who

dedicated verses to the future Edward V, Richard III and Henry VII's son, Arthur. The sons of William Haryot, the Mayor of London, entertained to a day's hunting in Waltham Forest by Edward IV, were merchants in Milan and finally became Milanese citizens, on Richard III's recommendation.

Alien craftsmen were common in London and many worked for the court and the great wardrobe, the department which made the king's clothes, horse gear, flags, banners and furnishings. Richard retained the services of George Lovekyn, Edward IV's tailor, a Parisian by birth, for some time. The painters who worked on his coronation were Christian Colbourne of 'Almaine' and William Melborne, an extremely prosperous painter of London. Painters of talent were available in London in the 1480s, whether English or from the Low Countries, and English painters collaborated, at the least, on the Eton Chapel wall paintings. Sir Thomas Thwaites was able to find one to paint an exquisite view across London from the Tower to Billingsgate and London Bridge to illustrate a copy of the poems of Charles d'Orléans which he proposed to give to Edward IV. An artist of equal talent was commissioned for the *Beauchamp Pageant*. For the best in manuscript and panel painting, however, the rich had to turn to the Low Countries: James III and his queen went to Hugo van der Goes but, if Edward IV or Richard III had their portraits done by a comparable talent, only later and poorer copies survive. William, Lord Hastings, ordered a lavish book of hours from a top Bruges shop in 1482–3, and Sir John Donne, his brother-in-law, commissioned an altarpiece from Hans Memling in 1477–80, and is associated with some finely decorated manuscripts. Beautiful painting was undoubtedly appreciated by Richard and his courtiers: many can be shown to have owned books decorated in London in the first twenty-five years of the fifteenth century, the last period of top-quality English illumination. Richard's own book of hours had one beautiful page in this style; his counsellor, William Catesby, owned the outstanding hours and psalter made for John Duke of Bedford; Richard's cousin, George Neville, Lord Abergavenny, owned a lavishly decorated book of hours, and his sister Anne, Duchess of Exeter, had a magnificent psalter. With such fine manuscripts available to them second-hand, many of them must have found it unnecessary ever to commission new, fashionable works of comparable artistry.

It remains doubtful how much either the Yorkist kings or their courtiers wanted all the luxuries and culture of the continent. Edward and Richard had spent brief, enforced exiles at the Duke of Burgundy's court and had first-hand experience of its protocol and ceremonies. A visitor from the duke's domains like Louis, Lord of Gruuthuse, could not complain of his regal treatment when he visited the English court in 1472 to be created Earl of Winchester. The hunting, dancing and courtesy were all up to standard, it seems, and Edward IV did not fear comparison when he showed him Windsor Castle, its park and his large and famous garden there which he called his 'vineyard of pleasure'. Olivier de la Marche, the master of ceremonies at the Burgundian court, visited England for the 1467 joust at Smithfield between Anthony Woodville, brother-in-law of Edward IV, and Anthony, the eldest illegitimate son of Duke Philip. His description of the event does not imply that it fell short of the standards of lavishness and organization to which he was accustomed on such occasions. He maintained contacts with England and sent a copy of his *État de la Maison ... du Duc Charles de Bourgogne,* a description of the ducal household, to Richard Whetehill, victualler of Calais, in 1474. He had a great respect for Margaret of York, 'Madame la Grande', the dowager duchess, and in the 1480s his lament for his dead masters and mistress made several courtly references to England. Despite the many diplomatic contacts and the continuous to and fro of merchants and artisans, the culture of England and its court remained essentially English, however, and not Burgundian. Even in something as apparently trivial as the iconography of books of hours, the decoration of the Hours of the Virgin and the Penetential Psalms usually showed the Passion of Christ and Christ in Judgement in England, and scenes from the life of the Virgin and of King David, respectively, on the continent.

HUNTING

RICHARD III was as anxious to preserve his hunting rights as any other medieval king and one of his most forthright orders on the subject went to his officers at Ware instructing them to reform the local inhabitants who had not only given up the approved, martial sport of archery for dice, bowls, tennis, quoits and other unlawful games, but were also destroying his 'hares, coneys, pheasants, partridges, herons, ewes and other, with engines contrary to our laws'.

Richard's great-uncle, Edward Duke of York, had translated *The Master of Game* by Gaston de Foix and no aristocratic education was complete without hunting skills. The English kings may not have held such intricately organized hunting parties as the Burgundian dukes, which lasted several days and included banquets attended by ladies, but they could lay on the most elegant entertainments for the Lord of Gruuthuse in 1472 at Windsor, when he was presented with a beautiful crossbow and the beasts killed during the day. The hunting party in Waltham Forest given by Edward IV for the mayor and aldermen of London in 1482 was hardly less elegant for they dined in 'a lusty and pleasant lodge made of green boughs' and were 'served right plenteously with all manner of dainties as they had been at London', the king waiting to see them served, and afterwards 'they course and course at red and at fallow deer, to their singular and joyous recreation...' Later, the king sent two harts, six bucks and a ton of Gascon wine to the mayoress, 'the which was shortly after eaten and drunken at the Drapers' Hall...'

The Setting and the Sport of the Court

ALTHOUGH BY THE END of the fifteenth century, England seems to have become increasingly dependent on painters and sculptors from the Low Countries for quality work, the native standards in building did not fall. Edward and Richard could draw on a particularly strongly established royal department of artisans with a tradition of skills under the king's clerk of works, his mason, his carpenter, plumber and glazier, each with their own yeomen beneath them. The greatest achievements of Edward IV that still exist today are

Windsor Chapel and the great hall at Eltham Palace. Richard built or planned to build extensively at Middleham, Barnard's Castle, York, Nottingham Castle and Warwick, but little remains that is firmly identifiable as his. He contributed generously to the pro-gramme of building King's College Chapel, Cambridge, which is probably his best memorial. Smaller gifts provided a Last Judgement window at Great Malvern and another window at Carlisle Cathedral Priory, but they do not survive. His mother-in-law oversaw the impressive memorial chapel for her father at Warwick, and his lord chamberlain, Francis, Lord Lovell, employed a top architect for his house at Minster Lovell, where he entertained the king in 1483. Apart from Edward IV's great hall at Eltham, the only other hall from the Yorkist period is Crosby Hall built by the London grocer, Sir John Crosby, and part of the house rented by Richard, when Duke of Gloucester. A fine and elegant building was the expected setting for a cultured aristocrat, even if only hired. Richard's choice of Crosby Place as his London house may have been the result of its chance availability, but it may also have reflected a pleased and deliberate choice — it was worthy of the Duke and Duchess of Gloucester.

Windsor, the centre of the Order of the Garter, was a place which provided everything a Yorkist king required: an impressive castle, a beautiful chapel in the latest architectural style of England, fine gardens and a park for the royal 'disport' of hunting. An elaborate array of officials, and the animals, parks and forests they looked after, enabled the kings and their court to hunt and hawk all over England. The greatest nobles and gentlemen held the most senior offices, the Earl of Arundel was Richard's master of game for all the forests and parks south of the River Trent and Sir Thomas Montgomery held this office in Essex. Beneath them there were local masters of game, parkers, keepers of otter hounds, hart hounds and hare hounds, of wild beasts, deer and coneys.

The king's personality could mark his court's culture as readily as his government. In two years, however, Richard III had little time to

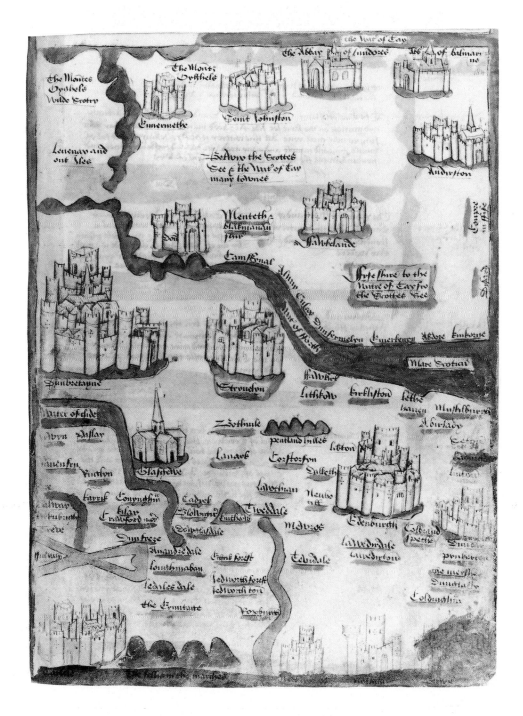

13 *A fifteenth century map of Scotland, from* John Hardyng's Chronicle. *Richard's raids against the Scots in the early 1480s gained him much prestige, particularly amongst ordinary soldiers.*

14 *James III, King of Scotland, with his heir,*
the future James IV.

impress himself as effectively on cultural activities as he did on his administration. The greatest barrier to our fully understanding the culture of either his court or his own tastes is the lack of household accounts. Perhaps he was too conventional in his tastes to make a mark. Conventionality, however, was not necessarily a bad thing in a king: subjects expected a king to be splendid, convivial, victorious and, above all, predictable. The display of Richard's court continued the pattern set by his brother and it continued to be an English version of the Burgundian model court.

The words of Richard himself and his secretariat are the best record of how they pictured a king and his court. One such image survives, in which the king is seen as the beneficent sun. The sun spreads and shares its warmth and splendour among the other luminaries of the sky and enables them to perform their subsidiary duties. The king similarly should share his power with his nobles and courtiers. Neither the sun nor the king can diminish his own power or pre-eminent position by this act of sharing. Richard and his servants considered themselves as well organized as God's natural firmament:

> It is good to see how the great sun itself, like a king seated in the midst of his nobles, and all the greater and lesser stars, each with its own particular light, illuminate the whole celestial court.

It is a very positive image and it was used in a very positive and happy document, the elevation of his son to the principality of Wales. As in the equally positive message to the Earl of Desmond with which this survey began, Richard III seems to have been very clear about his position as king and the role of his court. However fragmentary the evidence about the culture of his short reign, what does survive seems to present as positive an image. Richard committed himself wholeheartedly to the pursuits expected of a king and played the responsible role of the sun among his subjects with enthusiasm.

FURTHER READING

C. A. J. Armstrong, 'The Golden Age of Burgundy. The Dukes that outdid Kings,' in *The Courts of Europe. Politics, Patronage and Royalty 1400–1800*, ed. A. G. Dickens (London, 1977); *The Master of Game by Edward Second Duke of York*, ed. Wm A. and F. Baillie-Grohman (London, 1909); N. F. Blake, *Caxton and his World* (London, 1969); Otto Cartellieri *The Court of Burgundy* (London, 1929, reissued 1972); Sir John Fortescue, *The Governance of England*, ed. Charles Plummer (Oxford, 1885); Richard Firth Green, *Poets and Princepleasers. Literature and the English Court in the Late Middle Ages* (Toronto, 1980); *Richard III: the Road to Bosworth Field*, ed. P. W. Hammond and Anne F. Sutton (London, 1985); John Harvey, *Medieval Gardens* (London, 1981); *British Library Harleian Manuscript 433*, four volumes, ed. Rosemary Horrox and P. W. Hammond, (Upminster and London, 1979–83); J. Huizinga *The Waning of the Middle Ages* (1924, Harmondsworth reprint 1982); *The Household of Edward IV. The Black Book and the Ordinance of 1478*, ed. A. R. Myers (Manchester, 1959); *Richard III, Crown and People*, ed. J. Petre (London, 1985); Walter Prevenier and Wim Blockmans, *The Burgundian Netherlands*, trans. P. King and Y. Mead (Cambridge 1986); *English Court Culture in the Later Middle Ages*, ed. V. G. Scattergood and J. W. Sherborne (London, 1983); *Three Prose Versions of the Secreta Secretorum*, EETS.ES.74, ed. R. Steel and T. Henderson (1898); *The Coronation of Richard III*, ed. Anne F. Sutton and P. W. Hammond (London, 1983); Anne F. Sutton '"A Curious Searcher for our Weal Public": Richard III, Piety, Chivalry and the Concept of the "Good Prince"' in *Richard III, Loyalty, Lordship and Law*, ed. P. W. Hammond (London, 1986); Anne F. Sutton and Livia Visser-Fuchs, 'Richard III's Books,' in *The Ricardian*, volumes 7–9 (1986–93); Anne F. Sutton and Livia Visser-Fuchs, *The Hours of Richard III* (London and Gloucester, 1990); Anne F. Sutton, 'Order and Fashion in Clothes: the King, his Household and the City of London at the end of the Fifteenth Century' in *Textile History* (1991); *The Fifteenth Century, Proceedings of the 1986 Harlaxton Symposium*, ed. Daniel Williams (Woodbridge, 1987).

Chapter VI

RICHARD III AS A SOLDIER

Michael K. Jones

MILITARY TRAINING was an essential part of every medieval nobleman's education. He would learn the use of a variety of weapons (sword, lance and axe) and was expected to be proficient in horsemanship. Skill in arms formed the backbone of aristocratic culture. A reputation could be won through heroic deeds on the battlefield and just as easily lost through failure to fight for the interests of family, friends or servants. Noblemen were also required to display greater qualities: leadership and generalship. Man management was the most important political skill in the Middle Ages; its operation could be seen most clearly in time of war, when retainers chose whether to fight for their lord or to abandon him. For Richard III, the values and outlook of a military man had particular relevance. It was a code that lay at the heart of his own self-image, for which, ultimately, he would die courageously in battle. He thought and acted as a soldier, a perception that helps us to make sense of his political career.

Richard was proud of his family's military reputation. He played a prominent part in the reburial of his father, Richard Duke of York: a magnificent ceremony held at Fotheringhay in 1476. Richard, as Constable of England, encouraged the heralds to pay tribute to York's martial prowess at the end of the Hundred Years War. During his governorship of Normandy, it was recalled how 'he passed the river at Pontoise and drove away the French king.' The campaign Richard was referring to, that on the Seine and Oise in the summer of 1441, had represented a last chance of turning the tables on Charles VII.

His father's army came close to capturing the enemy monarch, an achievement that Richard held in high esteem.

York had been a vigorous champion of the 'military lobby' in the last years of the war. After his loss of office in France, he became a spokesman for those disillusioned by the final humiliating defeats in Normandy and Gascony. His empathy with the plight of ordinary soldiers and concern over the erosion of chivalric virtues were qualities extolled in a number of the chronicles of the war that Richard read and enjoyed. The only manuscript work known to have been commissioned by York, Claudian's life of Stilicho, told the heroic story of a great commander at the end of the Roman Empire struggling to reverse the tide of military fortune. Stilicho's efforts were brought to nothing by the machinations of a hostile court party. The work was begun for York late in 1446, when the malign influence of certain of Henry VI's courtiers had led to the rescinding of his second lieutenancy in France. It was a powerful exemplar. Richard had reverence for his father's name and never failed to reward families who had served him loyally. There can be little doubt that he was well acquainted with Claudian's work. He would have found it peculiarly apposite to his own situation in the early 1480s, when his own campaigning in the North was to be criticized by a hostile court faction.

The military reputation of Richard's eldest brother also seemed to rest on strong foundations. Edward IV was never to suffer defeat in any battle that he fought. His victory at Mortimer's Cross on 3 February 1461 inspired the badge of his dynasty, the sun in splendour; that of Towton on 29 March ensured him the throne. Richard had been too young to be present at these battles. Nevertheless, he keenly appreciated their significance, and was later to lay plans for an impressive memorial to the Yorkists who had died on the field of Towton, the bloodiest fight in the entire civil war. Edward IV also revived the prestige of the Order of the Garter, the premier order of chivalry. He kept the feast of St George (23 April) whenever possible and began building a magnificent new chapel of St George at Windsor from 1473.

Richard shared this enthusiasm. On the day of his coronation, he wore a long gown of purple cloth of gold marked with the insignia of the Order of the Garter.

Yet Edward was far too lazy to be a really good soldier. In the early years of his reign, when the Lancastrians were receiving Scottish backing and still posed a very substantial threat, he left the leadership of the dangerous northern campaigns to the Nevilles. His failure to head the Yorkist forces drew critical comment from even his closest supporters. William Lord Hastings wrote sardonically to a friend in the summer of 1463 that the king's enjoyment of the chase (an allusion not only to the hunting season, but also to Edward's insatiable sexual appetite, which was already becoming notorious at court) had distracted him from personally leading an army against the Scots. At a time of real crisis, in the spring of 1471, Edward IV roused himself, and his vigour and courage in the Barnet and Tewkesbury campaign won him back the throne. Then his familiar ways reasserted themselves. If there were sound diplomatic and political advantages in the abrupt termination of the French expedition of 1475, the king's lack of stomach for a tough campaign also played its part. Many felt his course of action dishonourable, and a chance to unite the aristocracy behind an aggressive, outward-looking war policy was lost. After 1479, when the truce with Scotland broke down, Edward was content to leave military operations to his younger brother Richard, just as he had relied on the Nevilles in the early 1460s.

Richard was devoted to the martial reputation of his father. His view of his brother's achievement was more ambivalent. Richard had served Edward IV loyally and, unlike his brother, George Duke of Clarence, he never conspired against him or engaged in rebellion. Yet comments made by Richard after Edward's death show that he was critical of the sexual excesses of king and court, which he equated with a lack of purposeful military leadership. There is evidence that in the second part of Edward's reign Richard openly disapproved of the king's conciliatory foreign policy. On one occasion, in 1474, Edward IV had to forcibly instruct his youngest brother to refrain from breaching the truce with Scotland. With this in mind, it is necessary to examine in more detail the military experience acquired by Richard before he became king.

How did Richard Duke of Gloucester assume the mantle of an aggressive military leader? His qualities first appeared during the dangerous and bloody campaigning of 1471. On 14 April, Edward IV defeated the forces of the Earl of Warwick at Barnet in a confused battle fought in a swirling mist. The nature of Richard's command during the engagement is not easy to determine. The possibility that he led the van of the army rests only on the assertion of a later source, *The Great Chronicle of London.* What is clear is that his conspicuous courage and disregard of danger encouraged his soldiers and impressed contemporaries. The chronicler Waurin described him bearing the brunt of the struggle alongside his brothers. The fighting was fierce. A newsletter written shortly after the battle by Gerhard von Wesel, a Hanseatic merchant living in London, reported that Richard had been slightly wounded. We also know that a number of his closest servants, grouped around his banner, died fighting that day.

Three weeks later, on 4 May, Margaret of Anjou's Lancastrian army was routed at Tewkesbury. It was a triumph for Edward IV's generalship and ensured his return to the throne. Here the evidence of Richard's role in the battle is more substantial. *The Historie of the Arrivall,* the only detailed contemporary account, relates that Edward gave his younger brother command of the vanguard. Richard acquitted himself with distinction. When Edward's main force faced a dangerous surprise assault from the experienced Lancastrian commander, Edmund Duke of Somerset, he kept his nerve. Determining on a bold and aggressive counter, he launched a flanking attack on the enemy position, allowing the Yorkists to turn the tables on their opponents. It was the decisive moment of the battle and, as a result of Richard's strategy, he and Edward together rolled back Somerset's line, which disintegrated in chaos. His prowess was duly noted in a poem composed to mark the triumphant return to London of the Yorkist army:

The duke of Glocetter, that nobill prynce
Yonge of age, and victorious in batayle
To the honoure of Ectour that he myght comens...

It is notoriously difficult to reconstruct the battles of the Wars of the Roses. Richard's bravery at Barnet and Tewkesbury, important enough in itself, needs to be placed in an overall context. He had remained loyal to Edward during the political crisis of 1470 and had shared his exile in Holland. During the campaign of 1471, he shouldered much of the military responsibility. When Edward was attempting to negotiate an entry into York on 18 March, it was Richard who commanded the Yorkist army outside the walls. After the victory at Tewkesbury, it was again Richard, as Constable of England, who presided over the execution of the leading Lancastrians. Aged only eighteen, he had rendered his brother stalwart service and could with some justification expect further opportunities to establish his military reputation.

The French expedition of 1475 offered Richard the chance of greater renown. His hopes were dashed when Edward quickly agreed terms with Louis XI at Picquigny. His opposition to the agreement was noted by the chronicler Philippe de Commynes. Commynes, present at the negotiations as part of Louis XI's entourage, reported how 'the duke of Gloucester, the king of England's brother and some other persons of quality, were not present at this interview, as being averse to that treaty.' Much had been hoped from this campaign. Letters from the English camp reveal the mood of excitement as Edward's army entered French territory. Thomas Stonor, writing from Guines on 19 July, fully expected a dramatic march on Paris and decisive engagement with the enemy: 'yf the frenchemen wyll do us the day, hyt shall not be longe or whe mete.' Similar sentiments were expressed by others as the army passed the village of Agincourt, the scene of Henry V's triumph sixty years earlier. But there was to be no battle. The agreement with Louis XI abandoned Edward's brother-in-law and ally, Charles the Bold of Burgundy, who had assisted his recovery of the English throne four years earlier. Richard's opposition showed that he felt this betrayal particularly deeply. Many humbler soldiers showed their distaste for the arrangement by joining Charles the Bold's army and continuing the campaign.

It is worth considering Commynes' remark that 'other persons of quality' were opposed to the treaty. The young Henry, Duke of Buckingham, is known to have withdrawn from the expedition and left for England with his retinue before Picquigny was concluded. It is likely that the intensely ambitious Buckingham was hoping to win lands and renown through war with France, just as his grandfather had, and had violently disagreed with Edward IV over the abandonment of the campaign. This would explain his subsequent puzzling absence from court (the brief exception being the trial of Clarence), his failure to gain office in the last period of Edward's rule and also his remarkable sense of common cause with Richard in April 1483, when he became his closest supporter.

For nine years after Barnet and Tewkesbury, Richard endured a frustrating lack of military activity. His opportunity finally came with the breakdown of relations with Scotland. After the collapse of the truce with James III, Edward IV appointed his younger brother lieutenant-general on 12 May 1480. Part of Richard's duties were defensive, preparing against the renewal of Scottish attacks across the border. But whereas in the early 1460s the Scots had held the initiative, from 1480 Richard took the war to the enemy. There is evidence of him leading a major raid as early as September 1480; in the following August he and Northumberland made an attempt to recapture Berwick. He was the leading influence behind a new thinking, aggressive and interventionist, that harked back to the successes of Edward III. The compact made with the disaffected Scottish nobleman, the Duke of Albany, in June 1482 owed much to Richard's prompting. His campaign in August reached Edinburgh unopposed, but the incarceration of James III by a group of his own subjects prevented a more dramatic success. Nevertheless, his forces were able to recapture Berwick. The military initiative had firmly passed to the English.

Regaining Berwick had a powerful symbolic value since it had been pledged by the exiled Lancastrian government to secure Scottish support for Henry VI: its recovery enhanced the prestige of the Yorkist dynasty internationally. Richard gained much credit from this period of campaigning, as the Italian Dominic Mancini, who had visited London in 1483, was to relate: 'such was his renown in warfare, that whenever a difficult and dangerous policy had to be undertaken, it would be entrusted to his discretion and generalship.'

Richard's actions as king's lieutenant in the North boosted his military reputation. His aggressive raiding policy was very popular and his forays into Scotland were recalled with admiration over a generation later, in Henry VIII's reign. Richard's concern that a major rebuilding programme begin at Berwick, including not only repairs to the castle and town walls, but also the construction of 120 new houses, shows his pride in the recapture of the town. His publicization of this success lies behind the remarkable royal grant of January 1483, vesting in him the county palatine of Cumberland. It was accompanied by the hereditary grant of the wardenship of the West March, the first time that a major military command under the Crown had passed outside royal control. In the last months of Edward IV's reign, Richard was preparing a new expedition against the Scots. A further reward was to be any part of south-western Scotland that he might afterwards conquer. Thus it was in Richard's interest to magnify his achievement in the North, to maintain Edward's commitment to an expensive war policy and the lucrative flow of patronage he was receiving as its result.

However, it would be unwise to overestimate Richard's military ability from what was, in broader strategic terms, a confused and difficult period of warfare. After a formal decision to invade Scotland had been taken by Edward IV and his council, in November 1480, substantial preparations were put in hand, Richard receiving £10,000 for the wages of his troops. The intention was to combine a land and naval attack, striking up the east coast of Scotland. Late in July 1481, John Lord Howard had appeared off the Firth of Forth with the main

English fleet. It was a considerable operation. Howard had 3,000 men under his command; his ships had been re-equipped with expensive artillery, bombards and brass handguns. The naval initiative was intended to support Richard's land attack but, for reasons that are not known to us, he was unable to move his troops in time and the opportunity was lost. The Stanleys were later highly critical of Richard's generalship, complaining that he failed to co-ordinate his forces effectively, and that their own contingent had been left isolated outside Berwick in considerable danger. Again, it is hard to substantiate their accusations, but Richard only concentrated the majority of his trooops for the siege of Berwick in October and little progress had been made in reducing the town by the end of the year.

In July 1482, Richard had headed a massive new army of some 20,000 men, accompanied by the pretender to the Scottish throne, the Duke of Albany. In the absence of any effective opposition, he reached the Scottish capital unopposed. His withdrawal from Edinburgh early in August 1482 provoked complaints that he had thrown away a great advantage. The *Crowland Chronicle,* a source particularly well informed on government affairs, attacked his conduct and lack of resolution, adding that the recapture of Berwick alone hardly justified two years of high military expenditure. It is not clear what else Richard was supposed to do in the situation, especially as most of his troops had been paid for only a month. However, the evidence does not justify the extravagant claims made on behalf of Richard's generalship by some of his admirers. Richard was at his best leading smaller-scale raids deep into Scottish territory, which he accomplished with verve and panache. It is here that his ability as a soldier has been underestimated. These plundering raids lay at the heart of border warfare and Richard conducted them frequently and effectively, from September 1480 to May 1482. His policy was highly popular among ordinary soldiers and his vigour and aggression helped to restore morale along the border.

This survey of Richard's military career reveals him as a brave and courageous warrior. His disregard of danger at Barnet and

Tewkesbury impressed contemporaries. His willingness to take the war to the Scots occurred at a time when Edward IV was failing to provide effective military leadership; Richard was prepared to take risks and fight. His initial opposition to the peace treaty with France in 1475 and his resumption of raids into Scotland in 1480 showed an understanding of the views of the ordinary soldier, a quality worth considering in more detail.

Richard was at home in the company of soldiers and respected their outlook. Two incidents are revealing. In June 1469 the royal entourage was passing through Norfolk. It was here that Edward IV learnt of a dangerous rebellion under Robin of Redesdale in the North and hastily began assembling troops and war materials. Richard was able to recruit men where others had failed, clearly on the strength of his own charisma. Thus he won over a number of John Paston's young acquaintances, 'waging' them to fight under his banner. A different kind of empathy is seen in his endowment of fellowships at Queen's College, Cambridge, in July 1477, when priests were commanded to pray for a number of Richard's relatively humble servants who had formed part of his following, grouped around his person and under his standard, and had died fighting with him at Barnet and Tewkesbury. Six years after their death, Richard still held their memory in high esteem and recalled their names individually. His attitude to these former servants went beyond contemporary notions of due reward and showed a keen personal regard for their welfare.

Richard cultivated a martial image. He was interested in the latest military equipment. In one contemporary depiction, he is shown wearing a tasset of scale armour (fabric covered in overlapping scales), still very much a novelty in the 1480s. He commissioned a copy of Vegetius's classical treatise *De Re Militari*, a famous manual also found in the library of Sir John Fastolf, a military adviser to Richard's father. Works like this were sometimes bought merely for display. In Richard's case, he strongly identified with its sentiments. One of Vegetius's famous dictums related that 'it is more wisdom and also more profitable to worke upon thyn own warriors and knyghtes than

Vegetius's *De Re Militari*

WRITTEN IN the late fourth or fifth century, this military handbook was to remain the soldier's 'bible' for more than a thousand years. Vernacular translations survive from the thirteenth century onwards. The following extracts are taken from the earliest, and most complete, English translation, *c*.1400.

Much of Vegetius's appeal lay in the way it encapsulated timeless common-sense platitudes, for example his frequent warnings against over-confidence and rushing into battle:

> For good leaders and wise chieftains will not lightly fight in pitched battle in open field ... instead with surprise assaults and ambushes they destroy the enemy with clever deceptions ...
>
> Never set out thy warriors or knights in battle array but thou have first tested them in three things: in long endurance of hardship, in deeds of arms in the face of an enemy's sudden onset, or in bold cheer in time of dread. In battles chance is all too mighty and so it is better to tame thine enemy by hunger than by fighting ... Good dukes never fight pitched battles in open field unless they have been driven to it by a sudden turn of events or by great need.

For the commander who had determined on battle, Vegetius was full of sound advice, whether on the importance of morale or on tactical dispositions:

> And at all costs beware that thou bring not a fearful or nervous host to pitched battle. Also pay not too much heed to the number and great multitude of thy people, but to their wisdom, strength, determination, and principally to their experience, for it matters less whether thy knights be

to hire othr tosande men in tyme of nede.' Richard shared this distaste for mercenaries. In May 1484, he told Nicolas von Poppelau, an ambassador from the Emperor Frederick III, that he would like to go on crusade 'with my own people alone'. In a letter of 11 August 1485, he poured scorn on Henry Tudor for relying on paid French troops to help him to win the throne. It was entirely characteristic that Richard's young or old as whether they have been too long at peace or recently active in war . . .

This chapter tells how thou shalt know the hearts of thy knights, whether they be inclined to fight or to flee. Therefore that day that thy knights should fight, take them before thee and ask them frankly about their wishes, and without any doubt thou shalt soon perceive and aspy, either by their cheer or by their words or their swift and hasty going or their slow moving and tarrying, which be bold and which be afraid. And in no way trust overmuch in the boldness of the newly recruited warriors for they that have suffered little in wars and have experienced but few perils, to such is fighting sweet and lusty, but such as have long tested the perils of war, they fear battle the more. Nevertheless, if the duke of the host is bold and hardy and determined on war, his good cheer and his comfortable words may make courage, strength, boldness and hardihood increase in his host, namely if he can show them any reasonable skill by which he may put them in trusty hope or comfort to have the victory. Therefore in this case it needeth that the duke comfort his people with good cheer and bold words, rehearsing too the falsehood of his enemy's quarrel and the right of his own cause . . .

Therefore thou that shalt be leader of an host in battle look thou set thy troops in so large a place that thou may move and turn all times of the day with the sun and have the sun and the wind on thy back and in thine enemy's visage.

But one rule look thou take most heed of that whether thou fight with thy right wing, or thy left wing or thy centre, set thy strongest and mightiest and wisest fighters that thou hast, both horsemen, footmen and archers, there where the burden and brunt of the battle will be. For victory and overcoming in battle is not in great numbers but in a few strong and wise and determined warriors, who must be arranged to best advantage.

prayer, composed for his personal use and copied into his book of hours, requested the intervention of St Michael, commander of the heavenly hosts, a soldier and a fighter.

Richard always honoured a military service performed for his family. He granted annuities, as king, to a number of those who had helped to recapture Henry VI in 1465, nearly twenty years earlier.

Such patronage was important in times of violence and uncertainty. It was an integral part of Richard's character and there is no doubt that men respected him for it. When William Lord Herbert drew up his will in July 1469, he made provision for those who had fought and died in his service. Similar sentiments were expressed by Henry, Earl of Nothumberland, in his will drawn up before Bosworth. If any of his men were badly wounded his executors were to maintain them in a 'convenient and reasonable fynding . . . for term of their life'.

The assessment of Richard so far has been a positive one, and rightly so. His qualities as a soldier enhanced his political success in the north of England in the second half of Edward IV's reign. His bravery and charisma were highly prized in this turbulent part of the realm and his advocacy of a return to the offensive against Scotland, evident as early as 1474, gained him considerable support. Richard's martial attributes helped him to forge a powerful new affinity from former followers of the Neville and Percy families. However, once he became king, far greater demands were placed upon him. A successful medieval ruler had to be more than an aggressive and energetic soldier. He had to offer a focus for the values of Crown and nobility to unite. In the late Middle Ages, the monarch was expected to be a chivalric figure, whether in feats of arms, inspired generalship or the ceremonies and ritual of the court. Malory, who composed his *Le Morte d' Arthur* in the midst of the Wars of the Roses, captured such needs in the mythical Arthurian court at Camelot. In 1484 Caxton dedicated to Richard his work, *The Order of Chivalry,* hoping that under the king 'the noble order of chivalry be herafter better used and honoured than it have been in late days passed'. Was Richard able to offer such a chivalric focus, to unite the English aristocracy behind him after a period of faction and internal rebellion, as Edward III and Henry V had done so successfully? It is a crucial question, and one that must be considered carefully.

Despite his proven ability as a soldier, Richard's martial experience was, in a number of respects, limited. Caxton's work had originally been intended for Anthony Earl Rivers, and the contrast between the two men is an instructive one. Rivers was a famous and accomplished jouster. His combat with the Bastard of Burgundy at Smithfield in June 1467 and with Adolf of Cleves in Bruges a year later won him great praise. He and other members of the Woodville family dominated the court jousts held in 1474 and 1477. Richard is not known ever to have participated in a joust, perhaps because Edward IV discouraged his brothers from risking the dangers of the tournament. Rivers had a greater pedigree of active military service. He had been given commands against France in 1468 and 1472 and may have fought for Charles the Bold at Morat in 1476. Richard's military career was, by comparison, a series of frustrated opportunities. The Milanese ambassador reported rumours, current late in 1472, that Richard was to lead an army against the French, but nothing came of it. A letter of Sir John Paston early in 1477 referred to speculation that he might be given command of an expedition to Flanders, again to oppose Louis XI, after Charles the Bold's death at Nancy. In the event, it was Lord Hastings who was sent to reinforce the Calais garrison. Although his letters of appointment as lieutenant-general in the North in May 1480 spoke of 'his proven capacity in the arts of war', the only campaign that he had taken part in was that of Barnet and Tewkesbury.

Richard was not yet nineteen when he fought for his brother's restoration in 1471. The following decade had given him little opportunity for any worthy martial exploit. Particularly galling was his lack of crusading experience, the most highly regarded path to chivalric renown. In December 1471, Anthony Earl Rivers was given safe conduct to go to Portugal, 'to be at a day upon the Saracens'. His young brother, Edward Woodville, was later to fight against the Moors in Granada. In January 1481, Edward IV considered sending a force to the assistance of the valiant knights of St John at Rhodes, who had already beaten off one Turkish attack. It was to be led by Rivers and Hastings. No place was found for the king's brother, and one wonders whether Edward discouraged him from participating. Richard's own wish to go on crusade was to emerge from a discussion with Nicolas von Poppelau, the ambassador of Frederick III, who

THIS WORK began life as Ramon Lull's late thirteenth-century Catalan *Libre del orde de cavalleria* before being translated into the French from which, as Caxton explains in the epilogue quoted here, he made his English version. Published in 1484, if it was seriously intended to inspire a revival of chivalry, it had to be dedicated to the reigning King of England and France, i.e. to Richard III. But who was the 'gentle and noble esquire' who commissioned the translation? And why was he not named? Perhaps because he was Anthony Earl Rivers.

> Here endeth the book of the order of chivalry which book is translated out of French into English at a request of a gentle and noble esquire by me William Caxton dwelling at Westminster beside London in the best wise that god hath suffered me and according to the copy that the said squire delivered to me . . . O ye knights of England where is the custom and usage of noble chivalry that was used in those days? What do ye now but go to the baths [i.e. brothels] and play at dice? And some not well advised and against all order of knighthood use not honest and good rule. Leave this, leave it and read the noble volumes of Holy Grail, of Lancelot, of Galahad, of Tristram, of Perceforest, of Percival, of Gawain and many more. There shall ye see manhood, curtesy and gentility. And look in later days of the noble acts since the conquest as in King Richard Coeur de Lion's days, Edward the First and Edward the Third and his noble sons, Sir Robert Knolles, Sir John Hawkwood, Sir John Chandos and Sir Walter Manny read Froissart. And also behold that victorious and noble king Harry the

visited him at Pontefract early in May 1484. When Poppelau told of the victory obtained by the King of Hungary against the Turks, Richard responded with some feeling: 'I wish that my kingdom lay on the confines of Turkey; with my own people alone and without the help of other princes I should like to drive away not only the Turks, but all my foes.' Richard's interest in crusading is also seen in his contacts with John Kendale, turcopolier (an officer of the Order of the Knights of St John) of Rhodes, whom he appointed to present his obedience to Innocent VIII, and in his patronage of the chapel of All Hallows,

Fifth and the captains under him, his noble brethren, the Earl of Salisbury Montagu, and many others whose names shine gloriously by their virtuous nobleness and acts that they did in the honour of the order of chivalry. Alas, what do ye do but sleep and take ease and are all disordered from chivalry. I would demand a question if I should not displease. How many knights be there now in England that hath the use and exercise of a knight? ... I suppose if due search should be made there should be found many that lack, the more pity is.

I would it pleased our sovereign lord that twice or thrice in a year, or at least once, he would do to cry jousts of the peace to the end that every knight should have horse and armour, and also the use and craft of a knight, and also to tourney one against one or two against two, and the best to have a prize, a diamond or a jewel such as should please the prince ...

Then let every man that is come of noble blood and intendeth to come to the noble order of chivalry read this little book and do thereafter in keeping the lore and commandments therein comprised ... And thus this little book I present to my redoubted natural and most dread sovereign lord king, Richard king of England and of France, to the end that he command this book to be had and read unto other young lords knights and gentlemen within this realm that the noble order of chivalry be hereafter better used and honoured than it hath been in late days past. And herein he shall do a noble and a virtuous deed. And I shall pray almighty god for his long life and prosperous welfare and that he may have victory of all his enemies and after this short and transitory life to have everlasting life in heaven where is joy and bliss world without end. Amen.

Barking, where the heart of the great crusading king, Richard I, was believed to be buried. It was certainly known to contemporaries. In the 'Ballad of Bosworth Field' his vow was dramatically portrayed:

King Richard smiled small
and sware by Jesu full of might
when they are assembled with their power all
I wold I had the great turke against me to fight.

Yet the practical experience did not match the sentiment. Although

107

a petition from the commons in the Parliament in 1484 referred to his 'princely courage' and the remarkable acts performed in 'diverse battles', Richard clearly longed for a great victory or enterprise that would establish his reputation.

The limitations of Richard's military career were important. They led to a gap between his martial self-image and his concrete achievements in warfare, between rhetoric and reality. If his abilities appealed to many ordinary people, especially in the north of England, more substantial qualities were needed to bind together the English aristocracy. Henry V had rallied the nobility behind him through the range of his military talent. He had served his apprenticeship during his father's reign in the Welsh wars. Here he had impressed observers with his skill in siege warfare, his grasp of logistics and his ability to co-ordinate naval and land operations. Richard's performance on the Scottish border was far more modest, leaving open the question of his real worth as a commander.

Henry V had come to the throne with a proven military reputation. Edward III had brought the nobility together through a different route, an instinctive understanding of the need for chivalric display and ritual at court. Here Richard was in a stronger position. Throughout the second part of Edward IV's reign, he had held the supreme chivalric office, the Constableship of England. He took his responsibilities seriously. He owned two rolls of arms and an ordinance composed by him in 1478 showed his interest in the heralds, urging the study of books of arms and the recording of ceremonies. It was Richard, 'in his own person', who dealt with the refusal of four new knights to pay the customary fee to the officers of arms. In 1484, he granted the heralds a charter of incorporation and gave them the London house of Coldharbour for their headquarters. Richard's patronage of the heralds shows that the chivalric code, the order and detail of military ceremonies, was important to him and he wished to see it properly enforced.

Unfortunately, the prestige of Richard's office had been seriously undermined. Edward IV had taken the controversial step of broadening the constable's jurisdiction to cover all forms of treason and disaffection. This had first been seen in the 1460s under John Tiptoft, and the measure was continued under Richard. In 1471 Richard, as constable, had presided over the trial and execution of Lancastrians captured in the aftermath of Tewkesbury. Two years later, he was involved in an altogether different matter, being empowered to investigate a dispute within the goldsmiths' company that was thought to involve treasonable intent. This extension of the competence of the constable's court beyond cases of treason which involved raising war against the king was arbitrary and unpopular. Nevertheless, Richard as king was to maintain the policy and his vice-constable, Sir Ralph Ashton, became notorious as an executioner.

Edward IV had never shown any deep respect for chivalric convention in the practical arena of politics. His pragmatism often shocked contemporaries and left a legacy of doubt and division. In March 1470, Edward had summoned Richard Lord Welles on the promise of a royal pardon. This was duly provided, but the king then chose to disregard his solemn oath and executed Welles on the morning of Lose-cote Field in front of the entire royal army. Such a breach of faith would have been unthinkable to Edward III or Henry V. It was in this atmosphere of ruthlessness that Richard was schooled. Contemporaries were soon observing similar attributes. The chronicler Waurin described Edward IV's efforts to get his army admitted to York in March 1471. When an angry discussion ensued between Edward, the Recorder of York and Martin de la Mer, Richard entered the chamber proposing to kill the burgesses and thus safeguard their exit from the city. *Warkworth's Chronicle* noted how Richard had executed the Bastard of Fauconberg at Pontefract in September 1471, despite the fact that Fauconberg had received a pardon from the king that summer. Both these accounts, composed in the 1470s, pre-date the distortions of later chronicle tradition and offer the earliest evidence of the darker side of Richard's character.

Richard's flair for bold and ruthless action was to serve him well in the spring and summer of 1483. He was able to assemble a powerful

Warfare and Chivalry

Thomas Malory served with the Earl of Warwick at the siege of Alnwick in the winter of 1462. It was one of the harsher actions of the Wars of the Roses. Winter campaigning was always unpopular and conditions in Northumbria were particularly bleak. John Paston wrote rather miserably 'no man can get no leave to go home [for Christmas] but if they steal away ... they should be sharply punished.' Yet Malory was to draw on his experience as inspiration for the heroic siege of Lancelot's castle of Joyous Garde in his *Le Morte d'Arthur*, a reminder of how chivalric values retained an importance in late medieval society. The following extract describes the fight between Lancelot and Gawain outside Joyous Garde:

> Then Sir Lancelot doubled his strokes and gave Sir Gawain such a buffet on the helmet that he fell down on his side, and Sir Lancelot withdrew from him.
>
> 'Why withdrawest thee?' said Sir Gawain. 'Now turn again, false traitor knight, and slay me, for and thou leave me thus, when I am whole I shall do battle with thee again.'
>
> 'I shall endure you, sir, by God's grace, but wit thou well, Sir Gawain, I will never smite a felled knight.'

retinue within two weeks of Edward IV's death and to surprise and arrest Anthony Earl Rivers at Stony Stratford on 30 April. His summons to his northern supporters on 10 June ensured a small but threatening army was bearing down on the capital when he was proclaimed king sixteen days later (the foot-soldiers were mustered at Finsbury on 1 July, but mounted detachments had reached London well before that date). A number of chroniclers stressed the importance of Richard's personal inspection and leadership of these soldiers: 'to be sure of all his enemies he sent for ... men of the north agaynst his coronacion, which came up and shewed themselves in Finsbury fielde, where King Richard received them, and rode with them throughe Chepe to Barnardes Castle'. There is no doubt that their presence intimidated many in the capital. Those whom Richard distrusted, such as Rivers and Hastings, were summarily executed. William Lord Hastings was an able soldier, highly regarded by his contemporaries, and his dramatic arrest and execution on 13 June shocked political opinion. Twelve days later Earl Rivers was beheaded at Pontefract after having been tried by a military commission drawn from Richard's own northern army: an act that was seen as arbitrary and illegal. Richard had established himself on the throne with speed and decisiveness. Securing the unity of his baronage was to prove more elusive.

At Bosworth on 22 August 1485, Richard faced Henry Tudor, his only serious challenger to the throne. It was the first battle he had commanded and one he should not have lost. Richard had the advantage of terrain and numbers, and was in a position to overwhelm Tudor's force. He took great pains to lead by example. The *Crowland Chronicle* recounted how he carried to battle the *preciosissima corona*, the 'rich crown' of England. It was a highly unusual but carefully thought-out act, typical of Richard, designed to encourage his troops. A contemporary Spanish report told how 'he placed over his head-armour the crown royal, which they declare to be worth 120,000 crowns, and having donned his cote d'armes began to fight with much vigour, putting heart into those who remained loyal, so that by his sole effort he upheld the battle for a long time.' Even sources hostile to Richard respected the gesture, seen in the defiant words attributed to him in one of the ballads emanating from the Stanley household:

> Give me my batell axe in hand
> and sett my crowne on my head so hye,
> for by him that made both sunn and moone
> King of England this day I will dye!

Richard's cause was to be undermined by treachery. Lord Stanley's substantial retinue had not joined the king's war camp and remained some distance away to observe the outcome of the conflict. Even so, Richard had enough troops to win the day. It was the failure of the Earl of Northumberland, one of his principal captains, to engage his forces that proved decisive. Northumberland's betrayal put Richard's whole battle line in jeopardy and forced the king's bold but desperate gamble, his charge against Henry Tudor's position and his efforts to cut down his rival. Richard came close to success, but his small contingent was intercepted and overwhelmed by the mounted men of Sir William Stanley, stationed on Tudor's wing. All were to praise Richard's courage in this last phase of the battle, even hostile sources. Polydore Vergil reported how he was killed 'fyghting manfully in the thickest presse of his enemyes'; John Rous that 'he defended himself as a noble knight with great courage to his last breath'.

Yet neither Richard's crown-wearing nor his bravery stemmed the tide of treachery that cost him the only battle he ever commanded. Stanley and Northumberland had fought with him at the end of Edward IV's reign and should have been his most stalwart captains. Richard's political ruthlessness and his breaches of oaths eroded the loyalty he had hoped to win and keep. Despite his undeniable courage, his empathy with the soldier's outlook and his flair for aggressive military action, he failed to show the higher qualities necessary for a chivalric reputation. He paid for it with the throne of England.

FURTHER READING

The standard background to Richard's military apprenticeship is found in C. D. Ross, *Richard III* (London, 1981). A positive reassessment of Richard's role in the war with Scotland is offered by A. J. Pollard, *North-Eastern England during the Wars of the Roses: Lay Society, War, and Politics 1450–1500* (Oxford, 1990). Important new evidence on the Bosworth campaign is provided in R. A. Griffiths and R. S. Thomas, *The Making of the Tudor Dynasty* (Gloucester, 1985). Opinion on the site of the battle has shifted from Ambien Hill to the plain below the village of Dadlington, half a mile to the south. The seminal article is Colin Richmond's 'The Battle of Bosworth', *History Today* (August 1985). For chivalric values in general, see Maurice Keen's *Chivalry* (Yale, 1984). Much useful additional material can be found in Pamela Tudor-Craig's catalogue of the 1973 National Portrait Gallery exhibition on Richard III.

Chapter VII

FOREIGN AFFAIRS UNDER RICHARD III

Alexander Grant

THE CONCLUSION to Professor Colin Richmond's important article, '1485 And All That, or what was going on at the Battle of Bosworth?' runs: 'What was going on at Bosworth in August 1485, therefore, was the fighting which ought to have taken place at Agincourt, or thereabouts, in August 1475.' The point is that for late medieval English kings good relations with the political community depended on victorious foreign warfare, as the reigns of Edward III and Henry V especially demonstrate. In 1475, Edward IV had the chance to emulate Henry V's example by reopening the Hundred Years War with France. But when he was confronted by Louis XI, near Agincourt, his nerve failed; he was bought off by the Treaty of Picquigny with a French pension worth £10,000 a year. Thus Edward IV did not channel the English nobility's aggressive instincts into foreign warfare. Instead, internal tensions were only superficially suppressed during his later years, and when he died the Yorkist regime collapsed in a welter of domestic rivalries. We cannot, of course, explain English politics in 1483–5 simply in terms of foreign affairs, but the argument is certainly thought-provoking, and provides a valuable background for the present essay.

For most of the Middle Ages English foreign policy had two main aims. One, applicable since 1066, was to defend, extend or recover the vast territories in France which belonged to or were claimed by the kings of England in conjunction, after 1340, with their claim to the

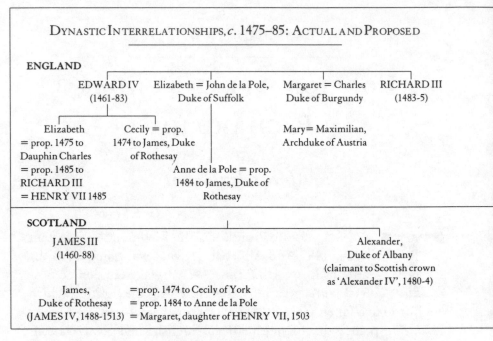

DYNASTIC INTERRELATIONSHIPS, *c.* 1475–85: ACTUAL AND PROPOSED

ENGLAND

EDWARD IV   Elizabeth = John de la Pole,   Margaret = Charles   RICHARD III
(1461-83)   Duke of Suffolk   Duke of Burgundy   (1483-5)

Elizabeth   Cecily = prop.   Mary = Maximilian,
= prop. 1475 to   1474 to James, Duke   Archduke of Austria
Dauphin Charles   of Rothesay
= prop. 1485 to
RICHARD III   Anne de la Pole = prop.
= HENRY VII 1485   1484 to James, Duke of
                                    Rothesay

SCOTLAND

JAMES III   Alexander,
(1460-88)   Duke of Albany
                                                                (claimant to Scottish crown
                                                                as 'Alexander IV', 1480-4)

James,   =prop. 1474 to Cecily of York
Duke of Rothesay   = prop. 1484 to Anne de la Pole
(JAMES IV, 1488-1513)   = Margaret, daughter of HENRY VII, 1503

throne of France itself. The other was to extend English lordship throughout the British Isles, which from the fourteenth century meant conquering Scotland. By the second half of the fifteenth century both aims had proved unattainable. In 1453, the last major piece of English-held territory in France was regained by the French; only Calais and its surroundings were left. And in 1460–1 the Scots captured the final English outposts in Scotland, Roxburgh and Berwick. At the beginning of Edward IV's reign, the English Crown had no land in Scotland and hardly any in France.

Was there, therefore, any reason why later fifteenth-century England should not have enjoyed good international relations? Powerful forces worked in that direction. Firstly, in the short term domestic politics were bound to take priority: internal stability had to be achieved before external warfare could be considered; meanwhile, good international relations would prevent domestic enemies from receiving foreign aid. Secondly, the English Crown could no longer afford sustained warfare abroad, chiefly because of a disastrous fall in

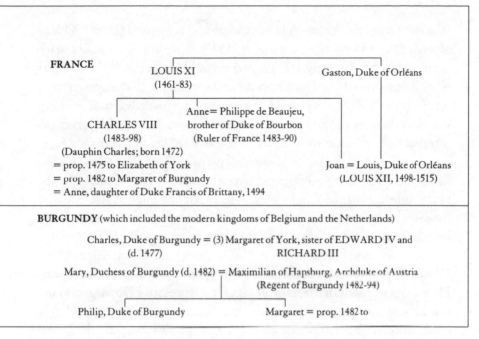

FRANCE

LOUIS XI
(1461-83)

Gaston, Duke of Orléans

Anne= Philippe de Beaujeu,
CHARLES VIII   brother of Duke of Bourbon
(1483-98)   (Ruler of France 1483-90)
(Dauphin Charles; born 1472)
= prop. 1475 to Elizabeth of York
= prop. 1482 to Margaret of Burgundy   Joan = Louis, Duke of Orléans
= Anne, daughter of Duke Francis of Brittany, 1494   (LOUIS XII, 1498-1515)

BURGUNDY (which included the modern kingdoms of Belgium and the Netherlands)

Charles, Duke of Burgundy = (3) Margaret of York, sister of EDWARD IV and
(d. 1477)   RICHARD III

Mary, Duchess of Burgundy (d. 1482) = Maximilian of Hapsburg, Archduke of Austria
(Regent of Burgundy 1482-94)

Philip, Duke of Burgundy   Margaret = prop. 1482 to

the customs on wool exports. Thirdly, England's former military superiority had ended: the defensive archer man-at-arms formation employed by Edward III and Henry V could now be defeated by the new, more professional French armies, which used guns and even artillery in battle. In these circumstances, it may not seem surprising that in 1474 and 1475 Edward IV made treaties envisaging lasting peace with Scotland and France respectively.

Foreign affairs, however, are never so simple. When Edward IV died, England was at war with Scotland and on the brink of war with France. Various factors made for hostility. As had happened in the past, Anglo-French peace left the English Crown free to resurrect English claims over Scotland; Edward did this in 1480 (setting up the exiled Scottish Duke of Albany as a puppet claimant to the throne of his brother James III), and in 1482 an English army entered Edinburgh and recaptured Berwick. The French, similarly, had little reason to trust English promises of long-term truce, for Edward still held Calais and styled himself King of France; there was no guarantee that the Hundred Years War would not be reopened (Louis XI had already had to buy off Edward in 1475). England's alliances with Brittany and Burgundy also caused difficulties because their rulers were being pressurized by Louis XI and sought English support; that undermined Edward's post-1475 peace policy towards France. There was also the constant irritation of Channel and North Sea piracy; as international tension mounted in the early 1480s, so the piracy escalated, with tacit government encouragement. Finally, there was the fundamental question of whether peace or war was actually in the better interests of the English Crown; as Richmond has stressed, the medieval English kings and nobility had more to gain from war — so long as it was successful — than they had from peace.

The last point would have been appreciated by Richard of Gloucester, whose career before 1483 suggests a keen aptitude for war. He was prominent in the later Wars of the Roses; in 1475, he provided the largest private contingent in the invasion of France, and was conspicuously absent from the peace negotiations; and he commanded the 1482 campaign in Scotland. His seizure of the throne is further testimony to his capacity for violent action. It would therefore have been a reasonable assumption that once Richard had consolidated his usurpation, he would decide to rally the English political classes behind him by waging vigorous war abroad.

That was, no doubt, his foreign image. After he became king, the rulers of Brittany, Burgundy and Castile all tried to involve him in military action against France. But hopes in Brittany, Burgundy and Castile would have been fears in France and Scotland. Philippe de Commynes' account of Richard's fury at the 1475 peace settlement probably reflects French perceptions of him. As for the Scots, they had seen him lead an army to Edinburgh and capture Berwick in 1482, and they must have known that in January 1483 Edward IV had authorized him to carve out his own private principality in south-west Scotland; when they wanted to flatter him at the Nottingham peace conference of 1484, they praised him as a triumphantly successful warrior. After 1483, moreover, the French (and presumably the Scots) considered him a murderous usurper. In both countries, therefore, Richard must have appeared a most serious threat.

Initially, however, Richard's actions appeared to belie those percep-tions. Exchanges with Louis XI and James III contained mutual as-surances of peace and goodwill. The Anglo-French truce was to be maintained, and a truce made with Scotland pending peace negotia-tions. Also, after Louis' young son Charles VIII succeeded to the French throne on 30 August, Richard reduced the Calais garrison, since 'the season of any great danger of adversaries is of likelihood over past for this year', and ordered negotiations for returning French shipping captured at sea.

But it was always dangerous to take Richard III's friendly words at face value. His attitude towards Scotland was not wholeheartedly peaceful. When James III proposed an eight-month interim truce, Richard, after a delay, only agreed one for two months; in November, James 'marvelled' that Richard was not more positive. As for France, despite Richard's assurances about the truce and his desire for peace, in late August 'the war is open between both nations', according to the Calais commander. And the main reason for reducing the Calais garrison was the 'other great daily charges resting upon us'; it was a cost-cutting exercise, perhaps in anticipation of domestic rebellion.

An 'open war' was taking place at sea. At the end of Edward IV's reign, his brother-in-law Sir Edward Woodville led English naval forces against a French fleet with a vehemently anti-English com-mander, the *maréchal* d'Esquerdes. In May 1483, Woodville fled to Brittany, but the war with d'Esquerdes continued. Shipping from Flanders (then allied with France) and Brittany also suffered increas-ingly from English attacks. On 30 July, bitter complaints were made to Richard that since May 'vessels of war of your said realm' had seized Flemish ships, 'and in all cases treat them as enemies'; while on 28 July, Richard authorized the arrest of Breton ships and goods to the value of £1,519, in retaliation for previous Breton piracy. There was a strong element of tit-for-tat at work, and no doubt the sea-captains often took their own private initiatives. But it was disingenuous of Richard to

RICHARD AND SCOTLAND, BEFORE APRIL 1483

DURING HIS BROTHER'S REIGN, Richard's role in the north of England naturally gave him an interest in Scotland. This may well have been personal interest, for he had a special devotion to St Ninian dating back to 1477 or even earlier; Ninian's shrine was at Whithorn in Galloway and his 'region' covered south-west Scotland and Cumbria. Be that as it may, Richard had been Warden of the West Marches since 1470, and when Anglo-Scottish warfare broke out in 1480 he was made lieutenant-general of the North. In 1482, he led some 20,000 troops into Scotland, nominally on behalf of Alexander, Duke of Albany, who had promised to accept English overlordship and surrender much of south-west Scotland. But although the campaign achieved the symbolically and strategically important capture of Berwick (lost to the Scots at the beginning of Edward IV's reign), it had enough finance to continue only for one month. Edward IV, who knew only the short Wars of the Roses campaigns, probably anticipated a quick battle (he may have thought that about France in 1475, too). In the event, the Scots would not fight; when, after a month, the English army's money ran out, Richard was fruitlessly besieging James III in Edinburgh Castle. The 1482 campaign, therefore, could hardly be described as a great success.

claim, as he did in instructions for his ambassador to Brittany in July 1483, that 'divers folks of simple dispositions, peradventure supposing that the peace had been expired by the death of the said king [Edward IV], fell to prizes and takings upon the sea.' He did suggest a conference to deal with the problem; but he was actually using piracy as a tool of foreign policy, which gave a cheap way of attacking any foreign power which seemed to threaten him. In Brittany's case, the threat lay in the shelter given to Woodville. The ambassador was instructed to

feel and understand the mind and disposition of the duke against Sir Edward Woodville and his retinue, practising by all means to him possible to ensearch and know if there be intended any enterprise out of land upon any part of this realm.

It was followed, in the January 1483 Parliament, by Edward IV's grant to Richard of Cumberland, together with as much land as he could conquer in south-west Scotland to be held as a virtually independent lordship, plus £10,000 towards his costs. The reasons for this remarkable grant are unclear. Edward might have wanted Richard to neutralize the Scots while he made war on France. Alternatively, it might have been Edward's response to Richard's likely complaints about inadequate funding in 1482; in future, Richard would foot most of the bill for Scottish warfare and would be recompensed from his conquests. Or, most intriguingly, was there an ulterior motive? Kings' younger brothers, without their own hereditary landed bases, almost always caused political problems; witness the Dukes of Clarence, Albany and Orléans. So is it possible that Edward IV, or perhaps Elizabeth Woodville, hoped to divert Richard's energies and ambitions beyond England into Scotland? In the early spring of 1483, that might have seemed attractive. Whatever the case, Richard himself was no doubt keen on the prospect of conquering south-west Scotland on his own behalf. Had Edward IV's death not intervened, he might well have tried to do so. But in that case, judging by the past history of Anglo-Scottish warfare, he would almost certainly have embroiled himself, and Edward IV, in an unwinnable Scottish war — and England's political history in the later 1480s would have been very different!

Here we see domestic concerns uppermost in Richard's mind, naturally enough. But he appears not to have realized that the best way to conciliate the Duke of Brittany, and so reduce the danger of a Breton-backed invasion, was to be seen to be tackling the piracy effectively. Richard, when possible, preferred to hit out rather than to conciliate. It is also significant that he feared a *Woodville* attack from Brittany; there was no reference to the other English refugee there, Henry Tudor. Richard simply did not seem to be concerned about him.

Duke Francis of Brittany, on the other hand, was well aware of Henry Tudor. On 26 August, he briefed his ambassador in a remarkable reply to Richard. Discussion of the conference on piracy would have to wait. More importantly, since Edward's IV's death, Louis XI

119

of France had been asking for Henry Tudor to be handed over. Francis had refused, because Louis would have used Tudor against England. Therefore Louis had threatened war against Brittany, in which Brittany would be defeated — and would have to surrender Henry Tudor — unless help came from England. Accordingly, Richard was to be requested to provide 4,000 archers for six months at his own expense and have another 4,000 standing by. In that case, 'the duke will await the fortune of war ... rather than deliver into the hand of the said King Louis the said lord of Richmond [Henry Tudor], or do anything prejudicial to the said king or kingdom of England.' It was explicit blackmail, which for the first time put Henry Tudor on the political agenda of Richard's reign.

If Richard agreed, he was to send sealed confirmation, which would ensure Breton friendship. That looks like a test for Richard — dating from shortly before the Buckingham rebellion. If so, Richard failed. Duke Francis equipped Henry Tudor's expedition to join the rebellion and subsequently welcomed him and many English refugees back to Brittany — where, on Christmas Day, Henry formally swore to marry Edward IV's heiress, Elizabeth of York. In late 1483, Brittany had become the greatest danger of all to Richard III.

Richard would have been well advised to make friendly overtures to Duke Francis, as Henry Tudor apparently feared. Instead, flushed with victory over the rebels, he chose immediate retaliation through naval warfare: not simply Crown-stimulated piracy, but as well organized a war at sea as was then possible. On 20 December, he was preparing for battle:

> For as much as the fleet of our enemies the Bretons now lying in Flanders intend upon wind and weather to depart briefly from thence homeward; we, gladly willing them to be met withall, have therefore caused divers and many of the ships belonging to us and this our realm to go to the sea to that intent.

It is uncertain whether the naval battle took place, but in the winter of 1483–4 government records contain many allusions to the war. Several flotillas were sent to sea, one under Lord Scrope of Bolton; sailors were recruited, English ships equipped, and a Spanish ship purchased 'to make war upon our enemies the Bretons'; while Breton ships, goods and sailors were captured by English captains 'of the king's armament'.

The target, however, was not only the Bretons. On 12 February 1484, 'certain of our ships of war' were being provisioned 'to resist our enemies the Frenchmen, Bretons and Scots': the war at sea against France had flared up again, as it also had (after the expiry of Richard's brief truce) against Scotland. Complaints about English piracy flooded in, too, from Flemings, Dutch, Germans and Spaniards; in the winter of 1483–4 Richard III's fleets were engaged in full-scale indiscriminate naval warfare.

This, not surprisingly, provoked his enemies to make common cause against him. Earlier French pressure on Brittany was replaced by encouragement for Duke Francis to support another Tudor expedition to England, and in mid-1484 a joint Franco-Breton fleet marauded victoriously in the Western Channel. Also, in early spring, a French embassy went to Scotland, and on 13 March the 'auld' Franco-Scottish alliance against England was firmly resurrected. Thereafter, French warships operated in the North Sea alongside the Scots — capturing two of Richard's best captains during the summer — as well as in the English Channel and Irish Sea.

Richard's 'most serious war ... with the very cruel and fierce people of the Scots' was originally intended to be waged on land as well. In February 1484 he was planning to attack 'our enemies and rebels of Scotland' the following May 'in person with host royal'. By April, however, he had changed his tune, and was asking for a Scottish embassy to be sent to him. But the Scots, aware of the other warfare with France and Brittany, were no longer interested in a truce which would leave Richard holding Berwick and also Dunbar (the Duke of Albany's castle, handed over in April 1483). Instead, Dunbar was besieged, while Scottish sea-captains joined enthusiastically in the North Sea war.

As with Brittany, Richard's reaction was retaliation. In the early summer of 1484, indeed, his priorities seem to have changed, towards waging 'the war at sea in the north parts' as actively as possible. One aspect was that East Anglian and Yorkshire fishermen had to sail to Iceland in convoys escorted by warships. And if the fishermen were affected, so too were the merchants of eastern England. Wool and cloth exporters and shipowners must all have suffered economically from the disruption of trade routes to the continent. The war in the North Sea was certainly not in the interests of Richard's northern and eastern subjects — as Richard no doubt was made aware, since he was in Yorkshire and the north-east from May to July. Here, he supervised his northern navy, which as well as fighting with the Scots was maintaining vital supply links with Dunbar. The greatest effort possibly came while he was in Scarborough, between 30 June and 11 July: according to the *Crowland Chronicle*, 'when concerned with maritime affairs right at the beginning of the second year of his reign ... near the town and castle of Scarborough ... he had remarkable success against the Scots.'

This victory probably ended the Scottish naval war because Richard followed it with fresh truce overtures, which James III accepted on 21 July 1484. But on 22 July there was a land battle at Lochmaben, east of Dumfries: the Duke of Albany had invaded Scotland, only to be defeated by local gentry. The Crowland Chronicler stated that 'many English' were captured, which historians have taken to indicate 'official English backing'; but there is no actual evidence of that. Instead, the raid's timing suggests it was a desperate effort by Albany to mount his own war in Scotland, following Richard's decisions to concentrate on the war at sea, treat Albany's castle of Dunbar as his own and finally make a truce with the Scots. This is confirmed by Albany's subsequent flight to France; he saw no prospects of help from Richard III.

Why did Richard cancel the land war against Scotland? He was shaken, in April, by the death of his only son and by rumours of another attempt on his throne by Henry Tudor and the exiles in Brittany. In

15 *Bernard Stuart of Aubigny, who probably recruited the Scottish contingent of Henry Tudor's expedition to England in August 1485.*

16 *Anne of Beaujeu, who as Regent provided the French backing for Henry Tudor in his invasion of England in 1485.*

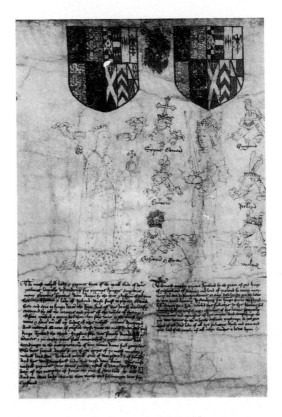

17 *A drawing of Richard III, made in his lifetime by John Rous, who undoubtedly saw his subject. It shows no trace of deformity.*

18 *Richard III, an engraving of 1677 from Francis Sandford's* Genealogical History of the Kings of England, *showing Richard as the tyrant king, with a symbolically broken sceptre.*

such circumstances he could no longer contemplate full-scale war in the north. Also, his 1482 army had largely consisted of northern magnates and gentry; but in 1484 many of these were employed to control southern England after the 'Buckingham' rebellion. They could neither campaign in Scotland, nor defend the north of England from Scottish counter-attack. Richard's use of northerners in the South precluded a land war against Scotland in 1484 — as Richard perhaps realized while in the region during the summer. Until the Tudor threat was neutralized and southern England reconciled to his rule, good relations with Scotland were essential.

Accordingly, a major peace conference was held at Nottingham on 13–21 September 1484. It produced detailed measures for dealing with piracy and cross-border raiding and agreed that James III's eldest son should marry Anne de la Pole, Richard's niece. Unlike the long-term peace agreed by Edward IV in 1474, however, the Nottingham treaty made only a three-year truce. The Scots may not have wanted anything longer, with Berwick and Dunbar in English hands; but it is also possible that the relatively short truce was the decision of Richard III, who subsequently prevaricated over the marriage. He perhaps expected that in three years Henry Tudor and the south of England would no longer be problems, and that he could then focus on Scotland once again.

Meanwhile, he had also finally decided that the anti-Breton piracy was counterproductive; good relations with Brittany were the best way to neutralize Henry Tudor. He probably proposed an end to the Breton war in the late spring, when his attention turned to Scotland. This was no doubt welcomed by the Duke of Brittany: ducal taxes on coastal shipping must have suffered, and an English invasion had been feared. In addition, Anglo-Breton peace was being urged by Maximilian of Austria, whose Burgundian subjects were also hit by the piracy. Therefore, on 18 June, a truce with Brittany was arranged (followed a week later by a ban on anti-Burgundian piracy); and Richard seems at least to have offered the 4,000 archers which Duke Francis had requested nine months earlier. The *quid pro quo* was presumably no more support for Henry Tudor. Faced with war on three fronts plus the Tudor threat, Richard was adopting more peaceful policies. But his earlier aggression had made the neighbouring rulers distrust him, and had established Henry Tudor as a viable rival. Was the change of policy too late?

The truce with Brittany and the offer of the archers were only initial moves in the effort to get hold of Henry Tudor, which in the late summer of 1484 must have been Richard's chief priority. What he needed was to persuade Duke Francis actually to surrender Henry, who had become an invaluable bargaining-counter. The Bretons, on the other hand, wanted to ensure that the promised English archers would actually materialize. Neither aim, we might think cynically, was a particularly likely prospect, given the past year's Anglo-Breton relations; in fact, by September both had come close to reality. In the event, however, the plans fell through, and instead a sequence of very different events began — which, ironically, led in the end to Richard's downfall at Bosworth.

The explanation lies chiefly in Breton and French domestic politics; in a sense, from August 1484 to August 1485 Richard III and Henry Tudor were both puppets in a continental political drama. In Brittany, where Duke Francis was ageing and ill, there was a conflict between the increasingly powerful treasurer, Pierre Landais, and various resentful Breton nobles. In France, meanwhile, Anne of Beaujeu, who with her husband was running the kingdom on behalf of her young brother Charles VIII, was challenged by a group of magnates headed by the heir-presumptive, her cousin Louis, Duke of Orléans. The two power struggles polarized: the disaffected Bretons received support from Anne of Beaujeu, while Landais formed an alliance with the Duke of Orléans. But Orléans was also making overtures to Maximilian of Austria and Richard III; he was trying to construct a great coalition, combining French magnates, Brittany, Burgundy and England, which would enable him to mount an irresistible rebellion against Anne of Beaujeu.

If Orléans were successful, it would have been in Brittany's interests (especially Landais') to have supported him. But it was risky for the Bretons to join in a French civil war without guaranteed English military support should Brittany itself be invaded. What both Landais and Orléans needed was for Richard III to join actively in the attack on Anne of Beaujeu, in return for which Richard required Henry Tudor to be handed over. One of Richard's right-hand men, (probably James Tyrrell) was in Brittany in September 1484, almost certainly negotiating both parts of the Anglo-Breton deal. Unfortunately for Richard, while Landais was organizing the force needed to seize Henry Tudor and his 400 or so fellow exiles, Henry was warned and fled to France where, in October, he and his companions were welcomed by Anne of Beaujeu and Charles VIII.

That transformed the situation. The idea of buying Henry Tudor out of Brittany by sending the archers no longer applied — and Tudor now had much more formidable supporters in the French regency government. For Anne, Henry Tudor provided a perfect means of threatening Richard III. She had good motives for doing so, English naval warfare against Brittany and Scotland might have ended, but it was still in full swing against France. More generally, the possibility of an English invasion of France, in conjunction perhaps with Brittany, Orléans or other disaffected French magnates, was still to be feared.

The French-backed Tudor challenge began with letters to England seeking support 'in the furtherance of [Henry's] rightful claim, due and lineal inheritance of that crown, and for the just depriving of that homicide and unnatural tyrant which now unjustly bears dominion over you'. Richard's response, on 7 December 1484, was a proclamation stating that Tudor and his companions, having had their 'unnatural and abominable' proposals rejected by the Duke of Brittany, had entered 'the obedience of the king's ancient enemy Charles calling himself king of France'. There, in order to obtain the 'support and assistance of the king's said ancient enemies and of this his realm' in pursuing his wrongful claim to the English crown:

[he] hath covenanted and bargained ... to give up and release in per-
petuity all the title and claim that the kings of England have had and
ought to have to the crown and realm of France, together with the
duchies of Normandy, Gascony, Guyenne, [and the] castles and towns
of Calais, Guisnes, [and] Hammes ... into the possession of the king's
said ancient enemies.

Furthermore, all Richard's subjects were ordered to be ready to
resist the said malicious purposes and conspiracies which the ancient
enemies of this land have made with the king's said rebels. Domestic
and foreign affairs had fused; Richard was connecting the threat from
Henry Tudor to the much broader issue of the defence of the realm and
employing rhetoric of the Hundred Years War to do so.

Despite Richard's obvious fears, it is doubtful whether the French
government could have managed any significant material support for
an expedition by Henry Tudor in the winter of 1484–5. By the end of
March, however, things were different. Early in 1485 the Duke of
Orléans mounted a rebellion, but gained little support; Landais, for
one, dared not to join him now that the offer of English archers had
fallen through. By late March Orléans had submitted ignominiously.
The French government now held the initiative, and the money and
troops originally raised to deal with Orléans were available for what
must have appeared a very worthwhile project: replacing the dangerous Richard III with a king who would be beholden to France.
Thus in the spring of 1485, while Richard was raising money and
organising troops for the defence of the realm, Charles VIII was
seeking his subjects' financial support (especially in Normandy) for
Henry Tudor — 'considering that he has the most evident right of
anyone in the world to the kingdom of England'. At least 40,000 *livres*
(about £8,000) appears to have been granted to Henry, and he was able
to borrow other amounts.

For Henry Tudor himself, meanwhile, news of Richard's rap-
prochement with the Woodvilles and idea of marrying Elizabeth of
York meant that in the summer of 1485 it was now or never. And two

other considerations may have been decisive. One is that (as Dr C.S.L. Davies has recently shown) in June 1485 Richard, no doubt reacting to Orléans' submission, at last made concrete arrangements to send archers (albeit only 1,000) to Brittany. But it was too late, for by the end of June Landais had been deposed and executed by his Breton rivals; all that was achieved was to intensify French fears of Richard's intervention on the Continent. The other concerns the bitterly anti-English *Maréchal* d'Esquerdes, who had been so prominent in the piracy war and was now in command of a new, expensive military base in Normandy which the government wanted to cut. It seems that D'Esquerdes, who later claimed responsibility for making Henry VII king, suggested sending many of the redundant soldiers with Henry to England.

That, together with the troops that Henry managed to recruit himself thanks to Charles VIII's financial support, meant that the Tudor cause had quite a substantial army. Contemporary figures vary, but Henry probably had at least 4,000 men with him when he sailed for England. Around 400 of these would have been the English exiles, but the majority must have been French — professional, experienced soldiers, drawn directly or indirectly from the newly established *gendarmerie*, and the kind of men who less than a decade later were to sweep through Italy with Charles VIII.

Henry's army also included a Scottish contingent of perhaps 1,000 men under Sir Alexander Bruce of Earlshall, according to one Scottish chronicler whose informant was Bruce's son; in 1486 Bruce received £20 a year from Henry VII for his recent 'labours' and a grant of land from James III for his service 'both inside and outside the kingdom'. The Scots had probably been recruited at the time of the Franco-Scottish treaty of March 1484 by Bernard Stuart of Aubigny, the commander of Charles VIII's Scottish guard. The implication of that, and especially of the subsequent reward to Alexander Bruce, is that James approved of this Scottish military action against England. Despite the Anglo-Scottish treaty of Nottingham, James, like the French, would no doubt have felt safer with a different king on the

FOREIGN AID FOR HENRY TUDOR

THE STANLEY-INSPIRED 'Song of the Lady Bessy' has the most blatant distortion of the French support for Henry Tudor:

Then answereth the King of France,
& shortlye answereth by St John,
no shipps to bring him ouer the seas,
men nor money bringeth he none.

Although Polydore Vergil's much more influential account is less extreme, it, more subtly, has a similar message — understandably, since it was produced early in Henry VIII's reign. Vergil made out that in 1485 Henry received much less from France in 1485 than from Brittany in October 1483. He described Charles VIII's aid as only 'slender supply'; stated that Henry left the French court and, on his own initiative, sailed 'with 2,000 only of armed men and a few ships'; and (unlike the Crowland Chronicler) made no mention of French troops in the account of Bosworth. In fact, French sources show Henry staying with the French court until shortly before his departure and receiving significant financial aid. Unfortunately, documentary evidence for the number of French troops provided has yet to be found. The Burgundian chronicler, Jean Molinet, however, recorded that Charles VIII provided 1,800 *compagnons de guerre*, and that another 1,800 were recruited just before Henry sailed. Similarly, Philippe de Commynes stated in one passage that Henry was given 3,000–4,000 men, paid for until they reached England; and elsewhere, that he had 'some 3,000 of the most unruly men that could be found and enlisted in Normandy'. Thirdly, a Castilian report told Queen Isabella in 1486 that Charles VIII gave Henry 2,000 soldiers, paid for for four months, and that

throne of England, particularly one who did not have Richard's interest in northern England and Scotland.

Henry Tudor's expedition to England in August 1485 was thus the outcome of anti-English policies by the French and Scottish crowns — indeed one of their most successful achievements, producing the King of England's death in battle and his replacement by their favoured he also had 3,000 English whom he found in France; subsequently, the commander of the French force was to take his 2,000 men into Castilian service. It may be concluded from these accounts that Henry probably had about 1,500–2,000 troops provided directly by the French government and recruited roughly the same number himself. The 3,000 English of the Castilian report were presumably the rest of Henry's men: his 400 or so English companions, the Scottish contingent and the other hired mercenaries. The totals tally reasonably with those given by the early sixteenth-century Scottish historian, John Mair: 5,000 men provided by the King of France, including 1,000 Scots. A later writer, Robert Lindsay of Pitscottie, also mentioned 1,000 Scots, under Alexander Bruce; while Pitscottie is a less reliable source, that figure (if not his 6,000 French and 3,000 English) is probably accurate.

Molinet stated that Charles VIII did not provide any of his ordnance, but Commynes wrote that Henry did have artillery; an artillery unit may have been among the privately recruited forces. Henry also had French gunners at Bosworth who, according to Molinet, advised him how to avoid Richard's artillery. This may help to explain the battle. The implication of Molinet's account is that the gunners advised approaching Richard's army from the flank; that would not only have taken the Tudor force out of the field of fire of Richard's artillery, but would have enabled Henry's own guns (perhaps a few small cannon mounted on carts, and almost certainly a number of hakbuts, or large handguns) to fire on the flank of Richard's vanguard. In those circumstances, the latter would have had to break its formation and engage in hand-to-hand conflict with the Tudor force — rather than picking it off at a distance with archery, as one might have expected. If that is what happened, then it echoes the victorious use of French artillery in the 1440s and 1450s, when the English were driven out of France.

candidate. Most English accounts of Bosworth, with Tudor- and Stanley-biased hindsight, play this down, but the truth is nearer the French propaganda claims that the Tudor dynasty owed its throne to Charles VIII of France. After all, arguably the biggest, and certainly the most effective and reliable, part of Henry's army at Bosworth would have been the French and Scottish contingents. And they surely would have made up Henry's vanguard, under the Earl of Oxford; the *Crowland Chronicle,* the only English account to mention foreigners, stated that Oxford had 'a large force of French as well as English troops'. Moreover, they were mostly professional soldiers. In earlier Wars of the Roses battles, smallish forces of English professionals from the Calais garrison were disproportionately influential; this would apply too to the larger force of French and Scottish soldiers at Bosworth. They would have been the men whom Oxford, according to Polydore Vergil, 'commanded in every rank that no soldiers should go above ten feet from the standards', and who then, probably wielding pikes in the style introduced into the French armies in the 1470s, pushed back Richard's vanguard in defeat.

Now it is that, rather than Richard's subsequent charge against Henry Tudor, which determined the outcome of the battle; had Henry's vanguard been defeated by Richard's, would not the Stanleys and other waverers have joined in on Richard's side? There is, admittedly, much that is unclear about Bosworth, but the crucial clash of vanguards was almost certainly determined by the superior fighting skills of Henry Tudor's Franco-Scottish forces. This reflects the new French military superiority, which had developed since the early 1440s, and which was to be seen so strikingly in Italy in 1494.

Bosworth, therefore, can be regarded as a French, or Franco-Scottish, victory, perhaps the ultimate revenge for the long history of English aggression against France and Scotland. This suggestion brings us back to the argument by Colin Richmond with which we started: 'Bosworth ... was the fighting which ought to have taken place at Agincourt ... in August 1475.' The response here must be that Edward IV *had* to make peace in 1475 because (as was pointed out above) the English crown could no longer wage successful foreign wars. Instead, French forces were able to fight victoriously in England and did so at Bosworth. Bosworth, to pursue the argument, *was* the late fifteenth-century counterpart to Agincourt — but it was fought in England.

Furthermore, this equation of Bosworth with the battles of the

Hundred Years War is not simply a military point. The themes of the present essay are mostly Hundred Years War themes: the English alliances with Brittany and Burgundy, the French alliance with Scotland, the interplay of Anglo-French and Anglo-Scottish conflict, the piracy, and above all the vital relationship between domestic and foreign politics, with rebels against one government invariably finding support from the other side. Foreign affairs under Richard III, in short, follow almost all the main patterns of the Hundred Years War.

Now, traditionally, 1453 marks the end of the Hundred Years War; but that date is due to English-biased hindsight. It was not until 1801 that the English kings stopped styling themselves kings of France. In the later fifteenth century, neither the French nor the Scots could be sure that the Hundred Years War was over — they had believed it to be over once before in what turned out to be only a lull between 1389 and 1415. If Henry V could resurrect the English wars in France, could not one of his successors? Edward IV tried to do so in 1475. And, it has been argued here, it was out of fears that Richard III might do the same that the French gave Henry Tudor their crucial support in 1485. In his response to that support, Richard claimed to be fighting in defence of the realm against its ancient enemy. He, therefore, presented the 1485 situation as an extension of the Hundred Years War. Was he so far wrong? Is there not a strong case, in fact, for regarding Bosworth not so much as a Wars of the Roses battle, but as the final battle of the Hundred Years War?

FURTHER READING
C. D. Ross, in chapters 10 and 12 of *Edward IV* (London, 1974) and chapter 10 of *Richard III* (London, 1981) gives the best general account of Yorkist foreign affairs. The main documents are translated in: *Letters and Papers Illustrative of the Reigns of Richard III and Henry VII* (Rolls series, 1861–3); *British Library, Harleian MS 433* (London, 1979–83); and Michael Bennett,

The Battle of Bosworth (Gloucester, 1985), appendix. My ideas were stimulated by Colin Richmond, '1485 And All That, or what was going on at the Battle of Bosworth?' in *Richard III: Loyalty, Lordship and Law*, ed. P. W. Hammond (Gloucester, 1986). Colin Richmond's 'English Naval Power in the Fifteenth Century', *History*, lii (1967) is also vital. For France and Britanny, see A. V. Antonovics, 'Henry VII, king of England, "by the grace of Charles VII of France"' in *Kings and Nobles in the Late Middle Ages*, ed. R. A. Griffiths and J. W. Sherborne (Gloucester, 1986); R. A. Griffiths and R. S. Thomas, *The Making of the Tudor Dynasty* (Gloucester, 1985) and C. S. L. Davies, 'Richard III, Brittany, and Henry Tudor', *Historical Research* (forthcoming: 1993 or 1994) — I am extremely grateful to Dr Davies for letting me use a proof copy of this most important article. For Scotland, see N. Macdougall, *James III* (Edinburgh, 1982), and L. J. Macfarlane, *William Elphinstone and the Kingdom of Scotland* (Aberdeen, 1985). For Burgundy, C. Weightman, *Margaret of York* (Gloucester, 1989). Michael Bennett, *The Battle of Bosworth* (Gloucester, 1985) and A. Goodman, *The Wars of the Roses* (London, 1981) are the most useful military studies; see also K. Fowler, *The Age of Plantagenet and Valois* (London, 1967), and P. Contamine, *Wars in the Middle Ages* (Oxford, 1984).

Chapter VIII

THE REPUTATION OF RICHARD III

P. W. Hammond

THE STORY of the reputation of Richard III is a long and twisting one. In some ways it has oscillated like a switchback, up and down regularly as the view of him changed from unfavourable to favourable and back again. Of course, the reputation of a person, the perception of their qualities, the relative esteem in which they are held, is not necessarily anything to do with their actual character, or their actions, but with people's perception of their character. Much may influence this perception. In the case of Richard III, it is pertinent to ask (as we shall see), how much did a knowledge of Shakespeare's play influence, wittingly or unwittingly, later writers on the king? Or did their political or religious beliefs influence them?

The Contemporary View
TO BEGIN at the beginning we may ask what his contemporaries thought of Richard of Gloucester (or such of them as recorded their views). Of course, as in any historical enquiry we will be drawing conclusions from documents not written for our purposes and care is therefore necessary in interpreting them.

We will start with those contemporaries who directly commented on his character. Of these the most valuable is a letter written in September 1483 by Thomas Langton to his friend William Sellyng, Prior of Christ Church, Canterbury. In this letter, Langton says:

He [the king] contents the people where he goes best that ever did
Prince, for many a poor man that hath suffered wrong many days hath
been relieved and helped by him and his commands in his progress.
And in many great cities and towns were great sums of money given
him which he hath refused. On my trouth I liked never the conditions
of any prince so well as his; God hath sent him to us for the wele of us
all.

Langton had just been made Bishop of St David's by Richard and
hoped for further promotion, so he was likely to be biased in his favour,
but the letter was a private one, and Langton would have no reason to
suppose that it would ever come to the notice of anyone else. He was
also an intelligent man with a high moral reputation. Hence the letter
probably represents a fair judgement that the king had a concern for
justice and for the welfare of his subjects, particularly the poor. It
also includes a Latin phrase which could mean that Richard (or his
followers) loved pleasure. Other favourable opinions were recorded
by the convocation of the provinces of Canterbury and York who
believed that Richard was of a 'most noble and blessed disposition',
and the University of Cambridge who saw him as kind and generous,
although this was after significant benefactions to the university.

A foreigner, Nicolas von Poppelau, who met Richard in May 1484,
referred in his travel report to Richard having a 'great heart'. He was
here attributing to the king the princely virtue of magnanimity, that
is a desire to do great things, particularly those benefiting the common weal. A feeling that Richard could be relied upon to carry out a
trust was probably felt by Earl Rivers when he asked Richard, as Lord
Protector, to see to the fulfilment of his will, made two days before his
execution in 1483.

William Caxton, in the Epilogue to his edition of *The Order of
Chivalry* (published in 1484) saw King Richard as likely to be inter-
ested in the book, and thus (presumably) as a chivalrous prince. John
Rous, in the English version of the *Rous Roll*, a history of the earls of
Warwick, drawn up in Richard's lifetime, described him as the 'good

NICOLAS VON POPPELAU

BORN INTO a family of Breslau businessmen, he entered the service of the Habsburg Emperor Frederick III and was knighted by him. In his own estimation he was distinguished both for the excellence of his Latin orations and for his dexterity with a lance so long and heavy that few others could even lift it from the ground. In February 1483, he set out from Vienna on a grand tour of Western Europe which was to last more than three years. According to his travel diary, he reached England in April 1484 and stayed some two months before sailing to Spain from the Isle of Wight. Besides visiting Richard III at Pontefract, where he commented on the beauty of the music, he spent about two weeks in London.

English cooking clearly left him cold, but what really seems to have impressed him was the forwardness of English women. He had only to enter an inn to find one of them offering to do for him whatever he desired. If he politely tried to shake hands with them, they insisted on kissing him. Moreover, he thought them remarkably beautiful — especially those from around Cambridge — and 'like devils once their desires are aroused. When they take a fancy to anyone they grow quite wild and blind with love, more so than the women of any other nation.'

As for the men, in his view, they matched the Poles for love of display and thievishness, the Hungarians for coarseness and cruelty and the Lombards for cunning and avarice. Yet, he observed, the English think they are the wisest people on earth and that there are no other people of any account in the world.

lord', punishing offenders against the laws and 'oppressors of his commons', gaining the love of all his people through his virtues. This echoes the remarks of Langton but, since Richard could reasonably be expected to see it, we might suppose that this was not entirely disinterested praise. Indeed, after Richard's death, Rous gave a very different description of Richard, as will be seen.

A rather similar eulogy to Rous's was written in 1484 by Peter Carmelianus, in the dedication of a poem to Sir Robert Brackenbury, Lieutenant of the Tower. This praised Richard's character in even more extravagant terms as prudent, wise, modest and generous. Like

The Fount of Justice

L IKE VIRTUALLY all rulers at all times, Richard wanted people to believe that he was deeply concerned to provide both strong government and swift and fair justice for all his subjects, rich and poor alike. After the collapse of the revolt of October 1483, for example, he had a proclamation declared in Kent which, after announcing measures to deal with the immediate aftermath of rebellion, went on to issue some splendid statements of principle:

> The king's highness is fully determined to see due administration of justice throughout this his realm to be had, and to reform, punish and subdue all extortions and oppressions in the same. And for that cause will that at his coming now into this his said County Kent that every person dwelling within the same that find him grieved, oppressed or unlawfully wronged do make a bill of his complaint and put it to his highness and he shall be heard and without delay have such convenient remedy as shall accord with his laws. For his grace is utterly determined all his true subjects shall live in rest and quiet and peaceably enjoy their lands, livelihoods and goods according to the laws of the land which they be naturally born to inherit.

These were clearly the proper sentiments, and government statements of this sort may have helped to shape the ways in which men like Langton and Rous chose to express their praise of Richard in 1483–4.

Although Richard rarely visited Kent — he spent ten days there in January 1484, and then another week in Canterbury in November — Kentish people, thanks to their proximity to London, had unusually good access both to the king himself and to the routine machinery of Justice.

Rous, Carmelianus also changed his mind when he addressed a poem to Henry VII. While these estimations of Richard's qualities were undoubtedly exaggerated and meant to please the king and his supporters, it must be said that they could not have been too outrageously untrue. If they had not been based on fact, no matter how tenuously, they would probably have had the opposite effect to that intended, and would have offended the recipients.

While Richard was king there were undoubtedly some people, how many we will never know, who distrusted and disliked him and thought him capable of acts of great cruelty. Dominic Mancini, an agent reporting on English affairs for the French, in a sober and detached account of affairs, said that after the young King Edward V was no longer seen in public, men believed that he had been murdered, obviously on the orders of King Richard. Mancini himself had no doubt that Richard was aiming at the throne from the moment he heard of the death of Edward IV, but this need be no more than what Mancini would have expected in his native Italy. His view of Richard's reputation was also necessarily based on the opinions of those in the circle in which he moved, since he was in England for just a few weeks (and indeed probably spoke only Italian and French, and Latin of course). His informants apparently saw Richard as deceitful and hypocritical, accusing Lord Hastings of a totally fictitious plot against his life in order to have a reason to execute him for his opposition to Richard's seizing the crown. Mancini's words would seem to show that at least some of Richard's subjects were willing to believe the rumours about him. We do not know how widespread this belief was, of course, and it must also be said that most rulers, no matter how good their previous character, would be believed by at least some of their subjects to be capable of committing virtually any crime. However, Mancini's picture of Richard III is not all bad. He writes that after the death of the Duke of Clarence Richard came rarely to court, but acquired a good reputation in his private life and his public activities, and was known for his discretion in undertaking difficult and dangerous tasks. There is good evidence that Edward IV accepted this estimate of his character and intended Richard to be protector after his own death. A final contemporary comment on Richard may be found in the pages of the York City Council Minutes. The councillors recorded their dismay that King Richard, 'late mercifully reigning upon us' had been 'piteously slain and murdered to the great heaviness of this city'. This seems to show that Richard had displayed only good qualities to York when he governed the North for his brother.

Decline and Fall of a Reputation

AFTER THE DEATH of Richard III, his reputation enters an entirely new phase. It is not now generally believed that the Tudors, through their historians, deliberately set out to blacken his reputation, but that they used materials already to hand. What is not in doubt is that these materials were heightened in tone, neglecting Richard's virtues and emphasizing his vices, and that new stories were invented, to point as great a contrast as possible between the character of the last Plantagenet king and the new Tudor dynasty which succeeded him. The reputation of Richard III reached its lowest point in the sixteenth century.

Rumours hostile to Richard were undoubtedly circulating before and very soon after his death. One of the earliest authors writing after the death of Richard was the Crowland Chronicler who wrote an account of events covering the life of the king. Whoever the chronicler was, and various names have been suggested, including that of John Russell, Bishop of Lincoln, who served Richard as his Chancellor, he undoubtedly had an inside knowledge of political events during the reign, and did not like Richard. This could have had something to do with the chronicler's dislike of anything associated with the North. He regarded Richard as a spendthrift, as deceitful and moreover as unjust. He does admit that he was a loving parent, however, in that he displayed much grief on the death of his only legitimate son, and that he was a brave man, dying like a 'spirited and courageous prince' at Bosworth. In thus recognizing Richard to have been a brave man, the Crowland Chronicler is supported by John Rous in his *Historia Regum Angliae,* finished after the death of Richard and generally hostile in tone towards him, unlike Rous's earlier work, mentioned previously. Even in this work Rous allows Richard to be generous. Another author, Polydore Vergil, accepted that Richard died fighting bravely 'in the thickest press of his enemies'.

Vergil is our first example of what may be termed a 'Tudor source'. He wrote his *Anglica Historia* about 1510 and was a humanist of international reputation. He was encouraged to write the history of

England, he said, by Henry VII, and his subsequent work has been described as intended to put a favourable interpretation on the rise of the House of Tudor. Richard's reputation suffers in the process. He is admitted to have been a man of considerable mental ability, but is also said to have been a dissembler and a hypocrite. All of his actions were designed to deceive the onlooker which, because people knew him, sometimes failed to have the desired effect. A charge of hypocrisy, common from now on when discussing Richard's character, is of course easy to make but difficult to prove, since it requires knowledge of a man's thoughts. Others writing at the beginning of the sixteenth century, such as Robert Fabyan in his *New Chronicles* and the London *Great Chronicle* also accuse Richard of being a hypocrite, of exhorting others to good and moral behaviour which he did not practise himself. *The Great Chronicle*, however, did regard Richard as an honest man in giving good and sufficient pledges to the city of London for the repayment of loans: an important consideration to a community of merchants. Fabyan and the writer of *The Great Chronicle* seem to feel that Richard was capable of ordering the murder of his nephews, but are unsure about other such acts, such as murdering Henry VI and his son Edward.

A picture was slowly being built up of a man capable of great evil, even if with some redeeming features. For example, as late as 1525 the aldermen of London protested to Cardinal Wolsey that Richard made 'good acts' (of parliament), i.e. had a concern for justice. However, in the *History of King Richard III* by Sir Thomas More, written in *c.* 1515, in what became the chief source for the reign of Richard, he is depicted as a man of ruthless villainy, with no redeeming features at all. This is not now regarded as history in the strictest sense — in a magnificent phrase Horace Walpole called More an author capable of employing truth as cement in a fabric of fiction. More's *History* is thought of now as little more than a treatise against tyranny, with Richard of Gloucester as the exemplar of the tyrant. Whatever More's reasons for writing his *History*, his reputation as a scholar, saint and martyr helped it to form the prevailing view of Richard for the following two centuries. In More's work Richard was evil incarnate. He was arrogant, cruel, above all a dissimulator, and had a physical appearance (i.e. a hump and withered arm, neither of which were mentioned by contemporaries) to match. His cruelty is shown in his responsibility for several murders, those of Henry VI and his son Edward, the Duke of Clarence, his own wife Anne Neville (this in order to marry his niece, later wife to Henry VII), and above all, of course, his nephews, More producing what became the authorized version of the death of the Princes in the Tower. There is no doubt that More invented details and 'improved' the story he received from various sources in order to increase its dramatic effect; moreover he admits that rumour was the only evidence for Richard's involvement in some 'crimes' such as his part in the death of the Duke of Clarence. More's *History* succeeded partly because it exploited the view of Richard III which had been developing in the previous thirty years, a view which suited the political needs of the Tudor dynasty. The requirements of Tudor propaganda do not explain why, after the death of the last Tudor monarch, people continued to believe in so unbelievable a villain.

This brings us to Shakespeare's *Richard III*. The play is the final culmination of the Tudor picture of the man who was Richard III, and is deservedly one of his most popular, dramatizing the Tudor view of Richard III in an unforgettable way. Shakespeare took this view and wrote a play about it, partly perhaps a morality story showing the abuse of power and the eventual rewards of tyranny, but mainly as a play, a great melodrama, to entertain. Shakespeare was not primarily interested in the historical truth of what he was saying, yet for many years it was taken as history. Marlborough is said to have remarked that Shakespeare was the only history that he had ever read, indeed, the influence of what was in essence More's assessment of Richard's character, reinforced by the genius of Shakespeare, lasted for many years and perhaps still does. It also fixed the image of Richard as a man whose evil mind was reflected by his bodily deformity. Thus, by the time Elizabeth I died, a particular view of Richard III's reputation had become fixed. As Professor Myers said:

by the end of the sixteenth century, the facts of his real appearance, character and deeds had been buried under a great mound of tradition. He became the archetypal tyrant-king incarnate and enthroned.

This was the view of him which prevailed generally for the next 200 years. We have, for example, George Baker, in his *Chronicles of the Kingdom of England*, describing Richard as 'born a monster in nature ... and just such were the qualities of his mind', and other standard histories, for example John Trussell (in 1636) and, at the other end of the period, David Hume (in 1762) had absolutely no doubt that the Tudor view of Richard III was the correct one. The following of the 'Tudor line', when any governmental pressure to conform had been removed, was largely due to the fact that the main sources being used for the history of the fifteenth century were now the Tudor chroniclers.

Signs of Recovery

SOME SEVENTEENTH-CENTURY authors did take an independent line. This formed a second strand in historical writing. George Buck wrote his *History of King Richard III* in 1619. This offered a complete defence of the king, scholarly in tone, in which Buck proved (to his own satisfaction) that Richard possessed all the virtues that a king should have, being moderate, temperate, merciful and generous. At the same time, even Francis Bacon, then Lord Chancellor, wrote in his *History of Henry VII* that Richard possessed the military virtues, was jealous for the honour of England, and a good law maker 'for the ease and solace of the common people', although his vices far outweighed his virtues. The latter were in any case 'fained' ones. Some of the eighteenth-century writers, Paul Rapin (in 1728), William Guthrie (in 1744) and Thomas Carte (in 1750) also did not wholly accept the traditional story, judiciously commenting on it, accepting or rejecting points as they seemed more or less plausible.

The most thorough-going defence of Richard III in this period was Horace Walpole's *Historic Doubts on the Life and Reign of King*

Richard the Third, published in 1768. Walpole, a gifted writer and amateur historian, followed Buck in many of his arguments, but his book was much more clearly and logically written, and also used a certain amount of new (and pre-Tudor) documentary material, which did not, however, always prove what he said it did. He successfully demonstrated that the Tudor writers on Richard III had not proved their case, they had merely asserted it. *Historic Doubts* was very popular, it went into a second edition the day after first publication, and had a wide influence among historians and the public. Several historians, for example John Wesley in his *Concise History of England* in 1776, and Malcolm Laing in his completion of Robert Henry's *History of Great Britain* in 1793, were convinced by Walpole's arguments. Wesley noted in his journal (in 1769) his amazement that historians should have swallowed the view of Richard III as a monster.

A More Balanced View?

AT THE START of the nineteenth century, there were thus two strands of thought on Richard III's reputation. Some authors, such as William Hutton in his *Battle of Bosworth Field* (second edition 1813), regarded Richard as a mixture of vices and virtues. Others, such as John Lingard, *History of England (1819–30)* were more traditionally minded and continued to accept the Shakespearian picture. However, the century was to see not only the beginning of a long-term change in the reputation of Richard of Gloucester, but the development of a more scientific approach to historical studies, aided by the publication of many original sources for the study of the fifteenth century.

The story of the change begins with the *History of England during the Middle Ages* by Sharon Turner which was published in 1823. In this judicious book, which is still worth reading, the author used original sources extensively, not merely reading and repeating the Tudor chronicles. He avowedly set out to adopt a more scientific and dispassionate approach to history and used this method to 'reduce the obloquy' under which Richard had remained to a just proportion. He found that the king possessed to the full the 'proud ambition', the 'unsteady temper' and 'fierce selfishness' of a fifteenth-century nobleman. Though he was physically brave, he was also a moral coward and, when he believed he was threatened, his response was to resort to criminal violence in the hope of averting danger. Thus Richard was, in Turner's view, guilty of the murder of his nephews. However, Turner cleared him of some of the other charges against him and believed that he possessed many good qualities. He was pious, a patron of both the arts and of lively intelligence, and his actions showed that he adopted a generally enlightened approach to his duties as king. This attitude towards Richard was followed by other writers, notably Caroline Halsted and Alfred Legge in biographies, and the list of qualities is something many historians would allow to Richard today.

However, some writers in the nineteenth century still continued to rely mainly on Tudor historians. Thus Agnes Strickland in her *Lives of the Queens of England* (1840) and *Lives of the Bachelor Kings of England* (1861) took an unqualified 'Morean' view of Richard's character. In the *Bachelor Kings,* the scenes are even dramatized. Strickland (and her sister Elizabeth, who wrote the relevant life of Anne Neville) did do some research into original documents, but discovered nothing new except, it would seem, Richard's extremely bad temper. Other authors took a more judicious attitude towards the character of Richard III, for example, John Jesse in his *Memoirs of King Richard the Third* (in 1862) and the constitutional historian William Stubbs (in 1878). These two authors took the view that More was probably correct, but that Richard undoubtedly had gifts in attracting popularity, being in addition resolute and clear-sighted as well as brave. This last quality is one which virtually no one, not even the Tudor writers, ever denied to Richard.

On the whole, as the nineteenth century progressed, Richard's reputation seemed to be improving slightly. But the pendulum swung back with the publication of the *Life and Reign of Richard III* by James Gairdner in 1878. Gairdner was a specialist in the fifteenth century, perhaps the first in the modern sense, and editor of many of the volumes of documents which were published. In his *Letters and Papers Illustrative of the Reigns of Richard III and Henry VII* (volume one in 1861 and volume two in 1863), he discusses the character of Richard III and in general takes a 'Morean' view in both, marginally more favourable to Richard in the first volume than in the second. Gairdner describes his attitude towards the study of history in the Introduction to his biography, explaining that tradition, in this case in the form of the hitherto received picture of Richard III, was essential to such study, since it provided the key to history.

In accordance with such views, the biography gives a picture of Richard which is strictly in accordance with the Tudor tradition. Virtually no act of the king is allowed to have any motive, other than a malign one, and he is portrayed as being capable of committing any crime of which he has ever been accused, although in some cases, such as the murder of Edward of Lancaster, Gairdner does allow some doubt. Richard is given some good qualities: bravery of course, generosity and piety to some extent, but the overall picture is as black as possible. The book was written with all the knowledge gathered through a deep study of the subject, but manages to reconcile this with a belief in the truth of the picture received from More and Shakespeare. He states categorically that 'a minute study of the facts of Richard's life has tended more and more to convince me of the general fidelity of the portrait with which we have been made familiar by Shakespeare and Sir Thomas More.' A trust in the value of tradition carried to excessive lengths, as Professor Charles Ross remarked, a trust perhaps exaggerated by Gairdner's conversion to Anglo-Catholicism in the year 1862.

Gairdner was followed extensively by historians, but his book also had another and rather unexpected result in the shape of an article in the *English Historical Review* in 1891 by Clements Markham, not a specialist historian, but an eminent geographer. A minute study of the events of the fifteenth century had convinced Markham not of the truth of More's and Shakespeare's view of Richard III, but of the exact opposite, that he was innocent of all crimes attributed to him. Richard emerged from Markham's article and from his subsequent *Richard III: His Life and Character Reviewed in the Light of Recent Research* (1908) as little less than a crowned angel, the exact reverse of the Tudor picture. Indeed, Henry VII emerges as the villain of the piece, either committing the crimes attributed to Richard, as in the murder of the sons of Edward IV, or causing the character of Richard to be blackened by hired writers. Markham's picture of Richard (which was attached by Gairdner in the pages of the *English Historical Review* and in the second edition of his biography) did very little for the reputation of Richard, since it was as little credible as was Gairdner's.

Richard as a Real Man Again

THE NINETEENTH CENTURY thus ended with Richard's reputation slightly improved over its lowest point, but with the 'traditionalist' view reiterated in what remained the standard biography of him for many years. After the publication of Markham's biography, there was a lull in Ricardian studies until the mid-1930s, when bones in Westminster Abbey, said to be those of Edward V and his brother, were examined by an expert anatomist and an antiquarian. These bones had been discovered in the Tower of London in 1674, in a place corresponding to where More had said the bones of the princes had first been buried. Such was the power of the More story that the bones were instantly attributed to Edward V and his brother — even though, again according to More, Richard III had subsequently ordered the bones to be moved elsewhere. The anatomist's conclusion that the bones could quite easily have been those of the Princes in the Tower and that they died in the reign of Richard III, reinforced the idea of Richard as a man capable of such actions, although the anatomical conclusions were disputed at the time, and have been ever since, chiefly on the grounds that neither date, age or sex were definitely established.

In 1936, the traditional view of Richard's character was further reinforced by the publication of the recently discovered report by Dominic Mancini. However, in an account of the Yorkist kings by

Those Bones

IN 1674, two skeletons of children were discovered in the Tower of London and immediately identified as the remains of Edward V and Richard of York. As such, they were placed in an urn in Henry VII's Chapel in Westminster Abbey. In 1933, they were exhumed and subjected to forensic examination by an anatomist and a dental expert, Wright and Northcroft. Their conclusion was that the bones were those of the princes and that they may indeed have been suffocated as Sir Thomas More has asserted.

Although the bones have not been examined since then, few modern medical scientists are willing to accept Wright and Northcroft's conclusions on the basis of the evidence which they presented in their report. Even if further examination using current techniques were to confirm the traditional identification of the bones, this would not help much unless it could also be proved that the children met their deaths after 22 August 1485. That at least would have the great advantage of putting the cat among the pigeons. (If it were proved they died before 22 August 1485, 'true' Ricardians would continue to blame other men for the murders.) However, there is at present no likelihood that radiocarbon or indeed any other dating techniques will be so precise within the foreseeable future. Until that happens, the bones themselves are best

Professor C. H. Williams in volume eight of the *Cambridge Mediaeval History* (1936), Richard is allowed to have been a man of his time, loyal to his brother, reasonably moral, pious and generous, and with a desire for justice, but also quite capable of acting in his own interest in seizing the throne and in having his nephews murdered.

After the lull in historical studies caused by the Second World War, the first serious biography of Richard III since that of Gairdner (or since Markham if his counts as a serious biography) was published in 1955. This was by an American Professor of English, Paul Kendall. It was certainly the first biography to seek properly to describe what 'manner of man Richard was, what manner of life he led ... Moral judgements I have left as far as possible to the reader.' The book

THE REPUTATION OF RICHARD III

forgotten. Nevertheless, the attitudes adopted to the bones in both the 1670s and the 1930s reveal very clearly how little prevailing opinion changed in the intervening centuries. According to the inscription on the altar in Henry VII's Chapel:

> Below here lie interred the remains of Edward V, King of England, and of Richard Duke of York. Their uncle Richard, who usurped the crown, imprisoned them in the Tower of London, smothered them with pillows, and ordered them to be dishonourably and secretly buried. Their long desired and much sought after bones were identified by most certain indications when, after an interval of over a hundred and ninety years, found deeply buried under the rubbish of the stairs that led up into the chapel of the White Tower, on the 17 July 1674 A.D. Charles II, most merciful prince, having compassion on their unhappy fate, performed the funeral rites of these unfortunate princes among the tombs of their ancestors, A.D. 1678, the thirtieth year of his reign.

In 1933, in a paper read to the Society of Antiquaries by the anatomist William Wright and by Lawrence Tanner, the archivist of Westminster Abbey, the authors concluded by expressing satisfaction that 'while the bones of Richard III have long since disappeared, trampled into common clay, those of the princes freed from all undignified associations rest secure, in the company of their ancestors, at the very heart of the national shrine.'

was based, again for the first time, as closely as possible on material contemporary with Richard. The character which emerged was an unfamiliar one, at least to the general public, of a man of justice and mercy, but still a man of his time and as such he was thought likely to have been capable, in the pursuit of what he judged to be his own best interests and those of the country, of such ruthless actions as ordering the death of his nephews.

In the years after the publication of Kendall's book, there was something of an explosion of scholarly research on the fifteenth century, not necessarily on Richard of Gloucester himself, but extending knowledge of events in his lifetime as never before. One outcome was the 1981 biography of Richard III by Charles Ross which presents a picture of Richard very similar in many ways to that of Kendall, albeit not so favourable. Ross's portrait is the one now accepted by most modern historians, with the exception of some Tudor historians, e.g. Dr A. L. Rowse, who seem curiously reluctant to abandon the Tudor picture of Richard.

Studies in recent decades have not been confined to professional historians. The character of Richard III is now of concern to far more people than ever before. Many novels are being written, perhaps instigated by *The Daughter of Time* by Josephine Tey, written from a 'revisionist' point of view in 1951; indeed, most of the novels are pro-Richard in tone. Many contributions to the discussion are being made by non-professional historians, e.g. by Jeremy Potter in his excellent discussion of Richard's character and reputation, *Good King Richard?*, and by the Richard III Society (of which Potter was chairman until recently), active for the last thirty-five years and containing professionals and non-professionals, which introduced modern scholarship to a wide membership and publishes important work on the period. The image of Richard that many but not all of these writers present is generally favourable in tone. Sometimes the authors allow their enthusiasm for one side or the other to run away with them, e.g. Desmond Seward in *Richard III: England's Black Legend* (1983) and Audrey Williamson in *The Mystery of the Princes: An Investigation into a Supposed Murder* (1978). The sheer number of these books, and indeed the four-hour 'trial' on television in 1984 (with expert witnesses and eminent barristers from the criminal bar prosecuting and defending), which reached a verdict of 'not guilty', shows that Richard III is a man whose reputation and character greatly concerns a much larger audience than ever before.

The Richard seen by modern historians (professional and amateur) was probably a genuinely pious and religious man. He certainly took seriously his coronation oath (to keep the peace, to do justice to all, to uphold the laws, and to support the privileges of the Church). He was a patron of learning and the learned. He was certainly a lover of music, an active man, courageous and exceptionally loyal to his friends. He was also a man who showed a certain lack of principle, although not necessarily any more so than did his peers, perhaps not very competent politically, and a man prone to anxiety. He was capable of illegal actions and the rumours that he had ordered the deaths of his nephews certainly began in his lifetime, soon after he took the throne. It is now accepted that there is no evidence of his being guilty of the other crimes of which he was once accused. Above all, he is seen as a man of his time, his character no better, but certainly no worse than his contemporaries. The character and reputation of Richard III thus comes full circle. As seen above, the contemporary view of him was of a man more or less the same as his contemporaries in his abilities, character and activities, although he does seem to have been disliked and mistrusted by some of them. His reputation plummeted after his death, partly for reasons more to do with the political climate than with his actual character, and he became 'evil incarnate', with a physical appearance to match. It then took 500 years to discard the accretions to his reputation given by the Tudor propagandists and to rely only, in Ross's words, 'on a close scrutiny of events themselves', in order to estimate Richard's character and hence to establish his current reputation.

FURTHER READING

George B. Churchill, *Richard the Third up to Shakespeare* (Berlin, 1900, reprinted Gloucester, 1976); Paul Murray Kendall, *Richard the Third* (London, 1955); Thomas More, *The History of King Richard III*, edited Richard Sylvester (Yale University Press, 1963); Alec Myers, 'The Character of Richard III', *History Today* (August 1954, pp. 511–521); Jeremy Potter, *Good King Richard?* (London, 1983); Charles Ross, *Richard III* (London, 1981); Anne F. Sutton, 'A Curious Searcher for Our Weal Public: Richard III, Piety, Chivalry and the Concept of the Good Prince', *Richard III: Loyalty, Lordship and Law*, ed. P. W. Hammond (London, 1983); Horace Walpole, *Historic Doubts on the Life and Reign of Richard Third* ed. P. W. Hammond, (Gloucester, 1986).

INDEX

ILLUSTRATION ACKNOWLEDGEMENTS

The illustrations on the cover and in the plate sections have been supplied or reproduced by kind permission of the following: Front cover, His Grace the Duke of Buccleuch and Queensberry (Weidenfeld and Nicolson Archives); 1, 2, and 3, Trustees of the British Library; 4, Geoffrey Wheeler; 5, Society of Antiquaries of London; 6, The Master and Fellows of Queen's College, Cambridge; 7, Northampton Museums and Art Gallery; 8, Geoffrey Wheeler; 9, The Treasurer and Members of the Bench of the Honourable Society of the Inner Temple; 10 and 11, National Monument Records; 12, Cuming Museum, Southwark (History Today archives); 13, The Bodleian Library, Oxford; 14, National Gallery of Scotland; 15 and 16, Giraudon; 17 and 18, Trustees of the British Library.